SHAKESPEARE'S HISTORIES & ROMANCES
IN EASY READING VERSE

By the same author:

Shakespeare's Comedies in Easy Reading Verse

Shakespeare's Tragedies in Easy Reading Verse

Shakespeare's Sonnets in Easy Reading Verse

Chaucer's Canterbury Tales in Easy Reading Verse

Charles Dickens' Oliver Twist in Easy Reading Verse

Charles Dickens' A Christmas Carol in Easy Reading Verse

Kenneth Grahame's The Wind in the Willows in Easy Reading Verse

SHAKESPEARE'S HISTORIES & ROMANCES
in Easy Reading Verse

Richard Cuddington

Copyright © Richard Cuddington 2005
www.richardcuddington.com

The right of Richard Cuddington to be identified as the author of this work has been asserted by him in accordance with the Copyright, Designs and Patents Act 1988.

This book is copyright material and must not be copied, reproduced, transferred or publicly performed or used in any way except as specifically permitted in writing by the author, as allowed under the terms and conditions under which it was produced or as strictly permitted by applicable copyright law. Any unauthorised distribution or use of this text may be a direct infringement of the author's rights.

Cover design by Denis Grigorjuk
Illustrations by Michael Avery

Published by CompletelyNovel.com

ISBN 9781849149549

Contents

The Histories
Richard the Second	2
Henry the Fourth Parts I & II	28
Henry the Fifth	70
Henry the Sixth Parts I, II & III	102
Richard the Third	156
King John	210
Edward the Third	228
Henry the Eighth	244

The Romances
The Tempest	264
Pericles, Prince of Tyre	292
The Winter's Tale	326
The Two Noble Kinsmen	360
Cymbeline	376

THE HISTORIES

'I challenge you, good sir'

RICHARD THE SECOND

Kings have many duties
That need attending to,
But dealing with high treason
Is one thing they *must* do.

And thus it was on one such day,
Richard the Second found
He had to act as arbiter,
He had there to expound...

And give a strong, sound judgement
And try to wisely gauge
The truth about a great dispute
That at the time did rage.

Henry Bolingbroke, the son
Of Lancaster's bold duke –
Arraigned a foe unto the king
And would not brook rebuke.

This was the Duke of Norfolk –
Thomas Mowbray, who now stood
Before the court and was accused
Of treason and falsehood.

Bolingbroke now made his case,
Mowbray he called a cur,
And threw his glove upon the floor:
'I challenge you, good sir.

'For you have been dishonest,
Misused our dear king's cash.'
Oh, how he ranted and then raved,
Oh, how his eyes did flash.

And then his anger boiled anew –
He called him an impostor,
And said, 'You are the one who's killed
Our much loved Duke of Gloucester.'

Mowbray denied this vehemently,
He said it was a lie.
He threw his glove down too and said,
'For that I'll see you die.'

King Richard hated this discord,
He liked things to be nice.
He pleaded with young Henry's dad
To give his son advice.

'My gracious Duke of Lancaster,
Please beg your son be calm,
Tell him to take his challenge back
For he may do much harm.

'And Mowbray, think again, good sir,
Of what you plan to do;
Fighting with bold Bolingbroke
Could mean swift death for you.'

Mowbray is determined
To duel for his good name,
And Bolingbroke declares that he
Intends to do the same.

He said, 'If I do less than this
'Twould wound my honour, sire.'
King Richard sees there is no way
That he can quench this fire.

And so with resignation
He declares that they must fight:
'Let chivalry determine now
Which one of you is right.'

Now this may seem straightforward,
But all's not as it seems,
For people think that Richard was
Involved in Mowbray's schemes.

They think that Richard secretly
Connived in Gloucester's end;
They think that Mowbray is the king's
Close confidant and friend.

So Richard –though he is prepared
Thus to support the duel –
Is really part of all the mess,
For he has helped to fuel...

The argument now raging,
And so he feels concerned –
The blood that's on his royal hands
Might somehow be discerned.

~ ~ ~

Later, the Duke of Lancaster –
Called John of Gaunt, by some –
Is having a hard time of it;
He's looking very glum.

The duchess of dead Gloucester
Is in an awful rage;
There are no words that he can find
To calm her or assuage...

The awful grief and wrath she feels.
She says, 'You are his brother.
You should demand revenge for this,
Far more that any other.'

But John of Gaunt averts his eyes
And solemnly looks down,
For he believes in monarchy –
He won't oppose the crown.

He'll not avenge his brother's death;
He will not ride roughshod
Against the king, for he believes
He's been put there by God.

The duchess feels let down by this
And vows – with tearful eye –
'In desolation I now leave
For home, and there I'll die.'

~ ~ ~

The story moves to Coventry
And in the morning mists
We spot the great arena
Wherein we see the lists.

And here the trial by combat
Is scheduled to take place,
With deadly weapons of the time –
The sword, the axe, the mace.

And then the mists evaporate,
The morning dew dries out,
And from the corner of the field
Comes an almighty shout.

'Long live the King! Here comes the King!'
And onto that vast field
King Richard rides with sword in hand
Along with his great shield.

He takes his place upon a throne
And then, with loyal zeal,
Mowbray and Bolingbroke approach:
Before the king they kneel.

They each declare their loyalty
To this their royal lord,
Heads bowed in supplication —each
With hand upon his sword.

And then the accusation
Is read for all to hear;
Then Mowbray's strong denial
Of this ignoble smear.

So now these enemies prepare
To test their strength and might.
But suddenly King Richard says,
'I'll not allow this fight.'

Everyone looked most surprised,
But Richard shook his head,
And showed that he was quite resolved,
For calmly he then said...

'I've changed my mind – it is my will,
It is my kingly right.
I've now decided both of you
Are banished from my sight.

'Mowbray, you will leave our realm
And nevermore return;
You'll never see this land again,
However much you yearn.

'And Bolingbroke, I banish you,
Though truthfully with tears;
Begone from this fair land at once —
For all of six long years.'

Old John of Gaunt was mortified
To hear his poor son's fate,
But hid his grief for he remained
True to the king and state.

And later on he says goodbye
To his departing lad,
And urges him to realise
That things are not too bad.

'For everywhere that heaven's eye
Does visit in a day,
Are happy havens for wise men,
And this I also say...

'Waste not your time in thinking
Of where you may have been,
But look ahead to where you go —
That future yet unseen.'

But Bolingbroke was not impressed
With all this clever stuff.
He left his dad and hurried off
In something of a huff.

~ ~ ~

Meanwhile, King Richard meets his court.
He says, 'Bold Henry shone
Within the heart of common folk –
I'm so relieved he's gone.'

But then he moved on swiftly,
For he had just had word
Of yet more strife and trouble
That had right then occurred.

He said, 'To this rebellion
In Ireland we must go.'
A courtier ventured, 'But my lord
Our funds have run quite low.

'It costs a lot of money
To run a decent court –
We'll have to raise the taxes.
I'll draw up a report...

'To show how it can be achieved,
And how your grace can get
An army to put down this foe –
We'll beat these rebels yet.'

But then news came that John of Gaunt
Was ill and nearing death.
Richard declared, 'Let's go – and hope
We miss his final breath.'

How very mean and callous!
But Richard now can see,
With poor old John's approaching death,
A way to get the fee...

That he must pay to raise a force,
To quell the Irish mob.
He rubs his hands and smiles and says,
'Well this is just the job.

'We'll grab his lands and property
Once good old John is dead,
But for the moment let us go
To visit his death bed.'

~ ~ ~

Old John of Gaunt is fading fast;
He sits there in a swoon.
Then he comes round and says to York,
'I hope the king comes soon.

'For I would have some words with him
And make him change his mind;
Show him the way to govern well
And leave his past behind.

'And I will tell the king the truth
And make my feelings plain,
For they speak truly who thus breathe
Their dying words in pain.'

The Duke of York sighed deeply.
'He'll not admit his crime,
Or any of his failings –
You'll only waste your time.'

But John of Gaunt will not be swayed
For he loves England so,
And says, 'I must speak out, dear York –
And shall before I go.

'For our beloved England,
Surrounded by the sea,
Has always seemed like Eden –
A paradise to me.

'This royal throne of kings,
This precious treasured isle,
I love each hill and valley
And each enchanting mile.

'For she is like a fortress
Within this silver sea,
Protected on all sides and safe
For all eternity...

'Against all foul infections
And cruel hand of war,
Envied by less happy lands
That lie beyond our shore.

'This earth, this realm, this England,
This womb of royal kings,
Famed by their birth and much renowned
For such courageous things.

'Acclaimed for deeds of chivalry
And Christian service too,
This land that's known throughout the world
For all that's good and true.

'This blessed home of such dear souls,
This dear beloved land
Is now leased out to one who has
A most unworthy hand.

'I love this blessed plot of ours,
This noble England here;
This dearest land, this sceptred isle,
And that is why I fear...

'For what will happen when I die...
If only England, brave,
Would vanquish scandal once these bones
Are laid within their grave.

'For then I'd die a happy man
And with my final breath,
Would welcome gratefully the hand
Of cold, ensuing death.'

Just as he finished his lament
King Richard walked right in.
Gaunt greeted him with scant respect
And with a sneering grin.

He then within a moment
Began a bold attack:
'You gild yourself with flatterers –
A vain, unwholesome pack.'

And then he let him have it,
For as his death was near
I guess it's fair to say he felt
He had no more to fear.

He told the king he was no good,
He really put him down.
He said, 'You are not fit to wear
Beloved England's crown.'

Richard wasn't taking this;
Old Gaunt had gone too far.
He said, 'I'd have your head chopped off
If you weren't who you are.'

But John of Gaunt would not be cowed.
He said, 'Your bile did foster
Ambition, which then made you kill
My brother, Duke of Gloucester.

'So let these words live when I'm gone,
And your tormentors be;
Let them ferment within your mind
As constant company.'

And then his head dropped forward,
And with a feeble wave,
He said, 'Convey me to my bed,
And thence unto my grave.'

Now shortly after this debate,
This monumental row,
The duke, despairing, passed away –
And Richard kept his vow...

To grab all Gaunt's possessions.
He just ignored the law;
He wanted all the wealth and lands
To help finance his war.

The Duke of York spoke out and said,
'This action is not fair,
For Bolingbroke owns all of this –
He is the rightful heir.

'And by your actions you will bring
Great danger on your head,
For this will mean you'll never more
Sleep easy in your bed.

'And I shall make a prophecy
That great disorder starts
From this time onwards, for you'll lose
All true and loyal hearts.'

~ ~ ~

Richard went to Ireland
To sort the rebels out.
He was confident he'd win –
Sure it would be a rout.

But Henry Bolingbroke has heard
Of how the king has taken
His lands and his inheritance –
He's very badly shaken.

Angry too, it's fair to say,
For this is quite outrageous.
But Henry is a bold, brave man;
He really is courageous.

And so he sails for England now
And brings an army too.
He's quite determined in his mind
On what he means to do.

He'll take the crown, for now he feels
For Richard mere contempt;
He'll end up king of England yet,
Or die in the attempt.

~ ~ ~

Richard returns from Ireland –
But he's delayed too long,
And by the time he gets back home
Affairs are going wrong.

Supporters have grown tired now
Of all this hanging round.
Within the realm, uneasiness
And discontent abound.

He is weak and doesn't like
The way things are unfolding;
He's really most unhappy at
The cards he finds he's holding.

Henry's forces gather pace,
They're gaining much support,
And as they win the people's heart
Poor Richard grows distraught.

His forces are in disarray;
It seems that victory
Will go to Henry Bolingbroke
Who promises to be...

A good and noble king to all.
King Richard's time is past;
It's time for England to be led
By someone strong at last.

It all comes to a head one day:
The king is safe inside
Flint castle, where he's made the choice
His court will now reside.

Richard says, 'I do believe
The waters of the sea
Do not have the power to wash
The holy balm from me;

'The sacred oil that marked me king,
That crowned me long ago;
I do not have to waste my time
In fearing any foe.'

But when Earl Salisbury came in,
His hubris was converted
To swift despair, when he was told
The Welsh had just deserted.

'Is now my kingdom lost?' he cried.
'Is this the end of me?
I am in truth then but a man,
Despite my majesty.

'For now it seems that we will pass
At once – with no delay –
From Richard's dark depressing night
To Bolingbroke's fair day.'

~ ~ ~

Henry's forces now approach —
Surround the castle walls.
And there it is the strangest thing
Quite suddenly befalls.

For first of all brave Bolingbroke
Says all he wants is this:
To have his wealth and lands returned,
Then he'll be pleased to kiss...

The royal hand of Richard there;
Call him his noble lord.
The king says he'll agree, of course,
To end all this discord.

But once this is agreed it seems
The king's will just breaks down;
He says he'll abdicate the throne —
Relinquish England's crown.

And asks, 'Will gracious Henry
Agree — and tell no lies —
To let me go on living
Until poor Richard dies?

'For then I'll give the crown to him,'
He said with furrowed brow.
'I will submit, I'll give my throne —
And I will do it now.

'I'll exchange my jewels for beads,
My palace I will give
For a humble hermitage,
And there I'll gladly live.

'My sceptre here shall be replaced,'
He said with weary laugh.
'By something more befitting like
A palmer's walking staff.

'And when I die, I humbly say
I really do not crave
A monument, just place me in
A modest little grave.'

So we can see that Richard thought
That he could never win,
And so he made his mind up then
To abdicate – give in!

A meeting then is organised
And, o'er a glass of wine,
King Richard, in dejection says
That he will now resign.

In one dramatic gesture
He makes this sad request:
'Bring me a mirror here at once.'
They think it is a jest.

But when the mirror's brought he looks
And says with tired groan,
'Is this the face that gazed upon
All others from the throne?

'It's hard now to believe it so,
For who would ever think
That, like the sun, this face did make
All rapt beholders blink?'

And then he dashed the mirror,
With anger to the floor.
'See how great sorrow wrecks a face;
I'll not look anymore.'

They asked him where he wished to go,
Where would he rest his head?
'In any place beyond your sight,'
Defiantly he said.

This angered Henry very much
And so, within the hour,
The former king was led away
And thrown into the Tower...

Where some time later, he was told,
'You're going to be sent
To Pomfret castle in the north.'
And that is where he went.

Richard was a sorry sight.
Is that what he deserved?
He may have been a weak, vain king,
For so we have observed.

And in reality 'twas this
That surely brought him down.
But should a feeble character
Cause him to lose his crown?

And there is worse to follow;
Things will be getting rough
For Richard, as King Henry
Has nearly had enough.

Then one day in court he cries,
So everyone can hear,
'Have I no friend who'll rid me of
This dreadful, living fear?'

Sir Piers Exton, who was there,
Is sure that this remark
Is Henry's plea for some good friend
To steal, when it is dark...

To Pomfret castle and there bring
A swift and certain end
To Richard – he believes that thus
He'll make the king his friend.

~ ~ ~

In Pomfret castle, Richard's held –
A prisoner now, we see;
He says, 'I wasted time before
But now time wasteth me.

'My hours are all faded
And it is very clear,
I had my day but now I see
That Bolingbroke's is here.'

And as he uttered these sad words
The prison door was flung
Wide open – 'What is this?' he cried.
A voice called, 'Hold your tongue!'

Sir Piers Exton then came in
With others at his side,
And Richard saw at once that they
Intended regicide.

He snatched a sword from one of them
And with a mighty thrust,
Sent the assailant to his death –
His face fell in the dust.

King Richard cried, 'Foul villain –
As you draw your final breath,
Know your own hand has thus supplied
Your instrument of death.'

And then he killed a second man,
And as the poor man fell
King Richard breathed, 'Go now and fill
Another room in hell.'

He fought them bravely, but, alas,
It was to no avail;
There was no place to run and hide
In Pomfret castle jail.

They hacked at poor King Richard
And with his dying breath,
He prophesied the injury
To England, by his death.

He cried aloud in agony,
'Exton, your foul hand
Has with the spilling of my blood,
Stained all King Henry's land.

'And so I say, rise up my soul
To heaven way on high,
While my gross flesh sinks downward now
Upon the earth to die.'

And then within a pool of blood
The wronged King Richard died,
A victim of his majesty
And of his kingly pride.

~ ~ ~

They took King Richard's body then –
A king without a crown –
To Henry at the castle keep
In royal Windsor town.

Exton told King Henry there,
'Upon this funeral bier,
I bring the lifeless body
Of your now buried fear.

'Here lies your greatest enemy,
Here lies the end you sought.
The scoundrel Richard's body thus –
Have I now hither brought.'

When Henry saw cold Richard there
His feelings were all mixed;
In some respects he was quite glad
The problem had been fixed.

But he told Exton angrily,
'I can't condone this plot.
It isn't what this king desired
And so I thank thee not.

'For by this deed of villainy
With your now tainted hand,
You've wrought a deed of slander on
My head and on this land.'

Exton cried, 'I did this deed –
Wielded my loyal sword,
Because I heard from your own mouth
You wished him dead, my lord.'

Henry sighed, 'It was not so –
Not what I meant,' he said.
'I didn't want him murdered, but
It's true, I craved him dead.

'And though I hate this awful deed,
I love him gone, and so,
I really can't complain too much.'
And he let Exton go.

And then he banished shamed Sir Piers;
He also made it clear,
That he himself was free of blame,
But, to allay his fear...

That he would one day rot in hell –
He vowed that he would go
Crusading to the Holy Land
Then everyone would know...

He'd wiped the slate entirely clean
For this horrendous thing.
He'd make amends for murdering
A true, anointed king.

And so although upset about
The murder in the north,
He'd ease his conscience and then rule
As King Henry – the Fourth.

He's a cunning rogue

HENRY THE FOURTH
Parts I & II

And so our story thus begins
That bears King Henry's name,
For he now sits upon his throne
Taking all the blame...

For King Richard's murder;
Shrouded all in gloom;
A melancholy monarch,
Henry sits there in his room.

He really is unhappy,
A very troubled king,
Weary and dispirited,
Borne down with everything.

For though he can't condone the way
Sir Piers rode roughshod,
And killed a king whom all had seen
Anointed once by God...

He still felt very thankful
To have Richard out the way,
And yet his thoughts convinced him that
There'd be a price to pay.

So as he sat reflecting,
His mood completely bleak,
He finally was moved to words,
And thus began to speak:

'I did not wish my cousin dead,
It isn't what I meant,
And for this dreadful murder I
Most heartily repent.

'Piers Exton made an error,
He didn't understand –
He's brought a deed of slaughter
On me and on this land.

'But now all this must cease, we'll heal
All gaping wounds and sores;
No more brother fighting brother,
We'll end these civil wars.

'And to wash away this blood
From off my guilty hand,
I'll make a pilgrimage this year
Unto the Holy Land.'

But as the king decided
That plans would now be laid
To travel to Jerusalem,
And make this great crusade...

Messengers arrived at court
And in a worried state;
They brought disastrous news, and so
Crusading now must wait.

Royal forces had been vanquished
By the Welsh and they had taken
Mortimer as prisoner;
The king was badly shaken.

For with Mortimer thus captured,
'Twas such a crushing blow,
But then another messenger
Declared, 'My liege, I know...

'Of happier news from Scotland,
Because I beg to tell
There's been a fearsome battle
Up in the north as well.

'But brave and daring Hotspur,
The king's most loyal friend
Has fought the Scots there hand to hand
And brought it to an end.'

'Bravo to Harry Hotspur!'
The king cried, 'Bring some wine,
We'll drink his health – oh how I wish
That worthy lad were mine.

'If only it were proven
That fairies did alight
Upon his cradle, when a child,
And in the dead of night...

'They'd swapped him for my worthless son,
So *he* was really mine;
That Harry Hotspur was my son –
And so the next in line;

'And not that useless reprobate –
My son, who's never here,
Who spends his time in taverns,
Quaffing wine and swilling beer.'

~ ~ ~

So having heard King Henry
Complain about his son,
We'll go to where this lad, Prince Hal,
Sleeps off a night of fun.

We find him at his lodgings,
He's there with his best friend;
A man whose great indulgences
Are truly without end.

I speak of Sir John Falstaff –
He's sixty and he's fat;
He has a bloated, ruddy face
And lots of ready chat.

He loves all forms of pleasure,
He's game for anything:
He likes the ladies of the night,
He likes to drink and sing.

There's hardly any silly prank
That Falstaff hasn't done,
And any moment of the day
He's up for having fun.

When his great booming laugh rebounds
Around a noisy room,
It causes all to laugh with him
And chases off all gloom.

He has a way of talking in
His deep and winning brogue,
That cleverly conceals the fact
That he's a cunning rogue.

For he is into thievery –
A bad example for
A royal prince of England
Who should respect the law.

Prince Hal should not be wasting
His precious time like this,
But hanging out with Falstaff is
A pleasure not to miss.

Now old Sir John is coming round,
He says when half awake,
'Whatever is the time of day?
Tell me, for goodness' sake.'

Prince Hal then chuckles merrily,
'Whatever do you care
What time the clock is telling
While you are lying there?

'Unless the hours are cups of wine,
The minutes food to eat,
And clocks the tongues of willing whores
You hope that you will meet.

'And the dials the signs of brothels,
The sun a gorgeous tart,
Dressed in a crimson, low-cut dress
And with a giving heart.

'If this, therefore, is not the case,
Then tell me sir, I pray,
Why in the world should you require
To know the time of day?'

Falstaff laughed out loud and said,
'You're not wrong there, my lad –
We thieves do all our work at night,
Not in the day, by gad.

'But when you're king, you'll have no truck
With thieves, I will be bound.'
'What none?' Prince Hal replied with mirth,
And made a mocking sound.

And so the banter carries on
In this light-hearted way,
It was the way they spent their time
On every single day.

But then another chap comes in –
Poins is this fellow's name –
And he takes but a moment
To join the verbal game.

He makes great fun of Falstaff,
He calls out, 'Hey, beanpole,
How go negotiations with
The devil, for your soul?

'You sold yourself Good Friday last
Just for a glass of wine.'
Falstaff laughed as if to say
That all was going fine.

Then Poins announced, 'I've hatched a plan
To make us all some dough
From pilgrims bound for Canterbury –
We'll rob them as they go.'

Falstaff cried, 'A great idea!'
Hal thought they'd come to grief
And strongly remonstrated,
'What me – become a thief?'

Sir John replied, 'Now come on, Hal,
And lend a helping hand.'
Prince Hal cried out, 'You know I can't,
You surely understand.'

Falstaff then became annoyed,
He said, 'I'll say one thing,
For this I'll be a traitor
When you become the king.'

He left them in a huff, but then
Once safely out the door,
Poins said to young Hal laughingly,
'Right, now I'll tell you more.

'For I've a mind to play a joke
On that bad-tempered lout,
And when I tell you of my plan
I know you'll fall about.

'We'll let fat Falstaff and his friends
Rob pilgrims on the pike,
But we'll stay safely out the way
And let them make their strike.

'For we'll arrange a meeting place
And then we'll fail to show;
They'll do the robbery on their own
While we are lying low.

'And once they've got the money
We two will then appear,
Dressed up in working clothes and masks –
We'll fill their hearts with fear.

'For they are cowards, one and all,
And so with no to-do,
We'll steal the money from them there.'
Hal said, 'We are but two!'

Poins cried, 'If that old bumbler,
That silly fool, that fraud,
Does not run off with all his friends,
Well then I'll eat my sword!'

Where was the fun in all of this?
Well, Poins went on to say,
'When we all meet at supper,
The rogue will find a way...

'To make himself a hero
When he gives us the gen;
He'll swear upon his life he fought
With over thirty men.

'He'll tell us how he drove them off,
He'll give it all a spin:
How many blows he suffered and
The tight spot he was in.'

They laughed out loud and heartily
Just thinking of the sight
Of their fat friend, Jack Falstaff,
On the ensuing night;

How he'd do everything he could,
Try every trick he knew,
To make his lying load of bunk
Appear completely true.

So then Poins said, 'Adieu, my lord.'
And left Hal all alone.
The prince's thoughts grew sombre
Now he was on his own.

He said, 'For just a little while
I'll go along with this,
And wink at all this nonsense
Though it is quite amiss.

'I'll imitate the glorious sun
Who lets the looming clouds
Conceal its beauty for a while
Behind their murky shrouds.

'So when it once again breaks through
In shafts of warming light,
Its very presence, that's been missed,
Becomes a welcome sight.

'Thus it will be with this fair prince,
For in a little while,
I'll put aside this worthless life
And moderate my style.

'And when this sudden change occurs,
When I improve my ways,
I'll be the meek recipient
Of much high-vaulted praise!

'For like a chrysalis, I'll break
And change my playboy past.
Then the world will all acclaim:
"He is a prince at last!"

'They'll say, "We knew it all along –
It was Hal's merry jest;
He is a proper royal prince,
The noblest and the best." '

~ ~ ~

While all of this was going on
There's trouble back at court,
For Hotspur and some others
Have now come south – but brought…

No prisoners along with them –
A most unusual thing:
It was the normal practice
To give some to the king.

Henry demanded prisoners
To ransom then for cash;
As Hotspur didn't bring them,
They were heading for a clash.

The king thinks artful Hotspur
Has other fish to fry;
He thinks that he is worried
That Mortimer might die.

You will recall that Mortimer
Was taken prisoner too;
Captured fighting for the king
As Henry rightly knew.

Welsh rebels held him captive,
But Henry wouldn't pay
A ransom for the Earl's release;
He had the nerve to say…

'It's clear he is a traitor –
He's guilty of great sin –
He should have kept on fighting,
Not simply given in.

'Why ever should I help him?
Now someone give me reason –
Why should I pay good money out
And why reward high treason?'

This made Hotspur wild with rage,
For Mortimer, you see,
Was brother to his own dear wife...
Of course, he wants him free.

The king thinks that he's trying
To do a crafty trade:
Mortimer for prisoners –
And that is what has made...

King Henry very cross with him –
His anger knows no ends –
So they became great enemies,
Who once had been good friends.

Henry, storming from the room,
Said in an angry fit,
'Send me all your prisoners
Or you will hear of it.'

Hotspur watched him go and said,
His face all taut and grim,
'Even if the devil roars
I'll not send them to him.'

And as he left the room he then
Decided on one thing:
To form alliance with the Scots
And then to fight the king.

What a different kind of youth,
What a ball of fire
Hotspur is compared with Hal,
For now he does conspire...

To take the throne of England;
His ambition does astound –
And all this time, all Hal can do
Is play and mess around.

~ ~ ~

A day or two have passed, and Hal
And Poins are now both waiting
Within the Boar's Head Tavern
To give Sir John a baiting.

Falstaff and his friends, as planned
Had stolen all the cash;
Then Hal and Poins attacked them
And made off with the stash.

So they expect old Jack's return,
And they can hardly wait
To hear just what he has to say –
But will he tell it straight?

Hal's in a right good humour
And has some fun awhile
With Francis, a young waiter who's
Respectful and servile.

Prince Hal reflects, 'I'm certain that
He's never been to school.
A parrot knows more words than him –
The lad is but a fool.'

Thereat this caused him to reflect –
He says, 'I'm not the same
As that wild fellow in the north
Who has the funny name.

'That fellow, Harry Hotspur,
So full of manly bluster,
Who's always boasting to his wife
And making her a-fluster.

'He says to her, "My darling wife
I have been out a-killing."
She replies, "Oh, Harry dear
That is really thrilling."

'He says, "I killed eight Scotsmen
While you were still in bed;
And there were many more of them
But they just up and fled." '

Thus young Prince Hal amused himself,
Inventing lots of fun
About young Harry Hotspur
And all the deeds he'd done.

Perhaps he was beginning
At last to be aware,
That people now were starting
To studiously compare...

The way he spent his princely days
With Hotspur – bold and brave –
And maybe they'd concluded now
That Prince Hal was a knave!

But at that very instant
There's banging on the door.
This is the moment that Prince Hal
And Poins have waited for.

In comes Falstaff with his friends.
Poins said, 'So how are you?'
'A plague on cowards,' Falstaff cries,
'And vengeance on them too!

'Give me a jug of wine, I pray,
My throat is dry and raw.
What is becoming of the world?
There's honesty no more!

'I know of only three good men
Unhanged in England now,
And one of them is fat and old.'
He pointed to his brow.

Prince Hal said, 'What's the matter,
You fat, old reprobate?'
'You're cowards, all,' Sir John replied,
Still in a fiery state.

Poins said, 'Don't call me coward,
Be careful what you say.'
The knight replied, 'Give me more wine,
I've had no drink today.'

Hal said, 'You drunken villain!
You've scarcely wiped your lips
Since knocking back your last huge glass –
I still can see the drips.

'But what's got into you, fat Jack?'
Hal asked his friend once more.
'I'll tell you, Hal,' John Falstaff said
'This morning, just we four...

'Set out and stole a thousand pounds,
We did it all alone –
Because you wouldn't join with us –
We acted on our own.'

Hal asked, 'So where's the money, Jack?'
Said Falstaff with a cuss,
'The cash was stolen on the road –
A hundred ambushed us!

'For two long hours we fought them,
It's amazing we're alive,
It really is a miracle
We managed to survive.

'See here, they stabbed me through my coat,
About eight times in all.
I've cuts in other places,
Too many to recall'

And so they bantered back and forth,
As Falstaff told his tale.
The more that Poins and Hal remarked,
The more he did regale...

The company about his guile,
How boldly he had fought,
How lucky his aggressors were
That they had not been caught.

He said they were a hundred,
But then he said sixteen;
It was very hard to tell
How many there had been.

Hal said, 'I do sincerely hope
That you ran no-one through.'
Falstaff said, 'I'm almost sure
That I put paid to two.

'Spit in my face, if you believe
That ancient Jack is lying,
But I saw two of them at least
Well on their way to dying.'

Sir John pursued with gusto
The details of the fight,
But Hal and Poins, of course, knew well
His words were false and trite.

So finally, Prince Hal came clean.
He said, 'You horse back-breaker,
You red-faced coward, hill of flesh,
You overweight old faker...'

But Falstaff interrupted with
A torrent of his own:
'You slimy eel, you ox's tongue,
You lump of skin and bone.'

But he ran out of breath, so Hal
Commenced his tale once more:
'It's time you knew the truth, old man
How we set on you four.

'And we saw how you carried on,
Just cowards, one and all,
And now you tell a pack of lies.
How have you got the gall?

We carried off the money
That you had seized, and saw
That you put up a lousy fight
When once you saw the score.

'Yes, *we* waylaid you on the road
And gave you such a fright.
The dreadful fear shown on your face
Was such a funny sight.

'And Falstaff, you old coward,
You took your guts away
About as nimbly as I've seen
In many a long day.

'We heard you roar for mercy,
You threw away your staff,
And ran with the dexterity
Of a sure-footed calf.

'So, my old friend, now let us hear
What clever lies you'll tell,
What explanation you'll advance
Of what we know befell.

'Come on, old Jack, speak up, we say,
For we can't wait to hear.'
After pausing, Falstaff said,
'Well, now, dear friends, draw near.

'Now listen very carefully –
I swear I knew you well;
I recognised the pair of you,
And though you did propel...

'Your friend who stands before you now
Into a grisly fight,
I do believe my actions were
Entirely in the right.

'For once I knew it was my Hal,
Once every doubt had flown,
You'd not expect me then to kill
The heir to England's throne.

'You know I am like Hercules
But even I would wince,
At thought of running through the heart
A noble, royal prince.

'I ran away through instinct, for
A lion won't attack
A prince – of that you can be sure –
And neither will old Jack.

'If I had acted differently
'Twould have been wrong and rash,
But let's get back to serious things –
I'm glad you've got the cash!'

~ ~ ~

Just at that very moment
Mistress Quickly hurried in.
She was hostess of the tavern,
This bawdy house of sin.

She said, 'My Prince, a messenger
Has come here from your father,
He's waiting here to speak to you.'
Hal told her, 'I'd much rather...

'That you would send him packing.
I have no wish to speak;
Send him quickly on his way
And give his nose a tweak.'

But Falstaff went to see him and
When shortly he returned –
There was no doubt that he was shocked
By everything he'd learned.

He said, 'That crazy fellow,
Harry Hotspur – whom you know –
Is raising a rebellion, and
Your dad wants you to go...

'To court first thing tomorrow,
For he is very sure,
The Welsh and Scottish rebels
Are planning to make war.

'He needs your presence with him.
The message is quite clear.
The king demands that you prepare,
To go to fight, I fear.'

They soon returned to jolly games
And merriment once more,
But then another knock was heard
Upon the tavern door.

It was the sheriff and his men.
'They want me!' Falstaff cried.
Prince Hal turned pale and said to him,
'You'd better go and hide.'

He hid behind a curtain as
The sheriff scanned the bar.
He said, 'We seek some robbers and
We know just who they are.

'One is quite notorious,
A fat man – likes his beer.'
'I can assure you,' Hal replied,
'He's not been seen in here.'

He sent the sheriff on his way.
'I'll do the best I can
To help you solve this robbery
And apprehend this man.'

They saw the sheriff to the door
And once they were quite certain
That he had really disappeared
They then drew back the curtain.

You'd think that Falstaff would be there
All cowering in a heap,
But this old drunken reprobate
Had fallen fast asleep.

He was sprawled out upon the ground,
And all he did was snore;
He didn't give a fig that he
Was wanted by the law!

~ ~ ~

As ordered, on the morrow morn
Hal took himself to see
King Henry in his palace, where
The king said, 'Leave us be.'

He spoke to all his courtiers,
He said, 'It's my desire
To speak alone, with my dear son.
I wish you to retire.'

And so the lords and ladies left,
They quietly withdrew.
The king turned to his son and said,
'What shall I do with you?

'It seems the very heavens
Turn their revenge on me,
By giving me a son like you
Whose manner's so carefree.

'For it is not appropriate
For one of princely rank
To carry on the way you do –
My son, I must be frank.

'You waste your time on base pursuits,
Your friends are all uncouth,
You are a disappointment –
I'm sorry, that's the truth.'

What in the world could Prince Hal say?
Yet, feigning mild surprise,
He answered, 'Some of what you hear
Are really downright lies.'

The king began a lecture,
He gave his son what for;
He said, 'Wherever will this end?
Your prospects look so poor.

'My friends all think you're heading
For an almighty fall,
And all we ever hear from you
Is how your life's a ball.

'You don't attend the council,
Your brother takes your place;
You never come to see me,
You never show your face.

'You mix with vulgar people,
Enjoy yourself too much;
You are forever showing off,
You lack the royal touch.'

Hal thought the king had finished,
He thought that he was done,
But Henry still had other things
To lay upon his son.

'Why can't you be like other lads?
You always let me down;
Even Hotspur acts with style
Though he now fights the Crown.'

This dressing down upset Prince Hal,
'One day, I'll prove,' he said,
'My honour is intact and true,
I'll bring you Hotspur's head.'

The king seemed satisfied with this –
How could he ask for more?
He said to Hal, 'Prepare yourself,
For we are now at war.'

~ ~ ~

And so two armies gaze across –
The one upon the other;
Once more a civil war looms large,
With brother fighting brother.

The word is out that young Prince Hal
Is quite a stirring sight;
He's all on fire for battle now
And ready for a fight.

Negotiations then take place
To try to find a way
To avoid a bloody clash,
And so not fight that day.

Prince Hal suggests a daring scheme:
'This Hotspur,' he then said,
'I'll fight in single combat and
Will spare all this bloodshed.

'The winner claims the victory
Of the battle here today.
I know that I can beat him,
My lord, what do you say?'

King Henry would have none of it.
He spoke up with a frown:
'You must be joking, I'll not risk
The forfeit of my crown...

'On you, an inexperienced boy –
It really wouldn't do –
For Hotspur, in a moment, would
Make mincemeat out of you.'

All parleying came to an end,
It was now time to fight;
Two armies faced the great divide,
A truly fearful sight.

And then the battle started,
And so without delay,
It turned into a raging scene;
A tangled, massive fray.

Prince Hal was badly wounded
But didn't think to yield;
Despite his bleeding, gaping wound
He would not leave the field.

He went back into battle and
He found King Henry there,
Fighting with Earl Douglas;
Hal cried, 'Come, if you dare...

'And cross your sword with me, proud Earl;
I swear I'll run you through,
For it is Harry, Prince of Wales,
Whom you are talking to.'

They fought – but then Earl Douglas
Turned on his tail and ran;
A cowardly example from
A so-called gentleman.

King Henry was extremely pleased
With what the prince had done,
He said, 'You have redeemed yourself;
I'm proud of you, my son.'

The king retired from the scene –
And then it was quite weird –
For almost out of nowhere
Bold Hotspur now appeared.

He said to Hal, 'I do believe
You're Harry, Prince of Wales,
And I am Harry Hotspur,
Of whom you've heard some tales.

'The time has come for one of us
To leave this blessed earth,
So let us cross our swords to find
The measure of our worth.'

Prince Hal replied, 'So be it, for
Two stars can't occupy
The selfsame orbit high above,
So one of us must die.'

As they began their fearsome fight
A friend came on the scene:
'Twas fat and foolish Falstaff –
Whatever did this mean?

Well, he had joined the army,
To fight there in the war;
He'd thought that it would be a lark,
He'd have some fun for sure.

Falstaff cheered his friend, the prince,
He yelled, 'Go on – attack!'
But as he urged him on, behold!
Earl Douglas came on back.

Then they began to fight as well.
'I don't like this,' Jack said,
And so he fell onto the ground
Pretending to be dead.

Douglas hurried on his way;
Prince Hal –with one deft thrust –
Gave Hotspur such a mortal wound
He fell down in the dust.

'Hal, you've robbed me of my youth,'
He cried, 'But what hurts most
Is that you take all honours.'
Then he gave up the ghost.

Hal looked down upon the corpse –
'Farewell, brave heart,' he said.
'A kingdom was too small for you
Before you lay there dead;

'But now, my lord, because of this
Bloody, hard fought deed,
A plot of just six feet of earth
Is all that you will need.

'So farewell, Harry Hotspur,
You were valiant, for sure.'
Then turning round he saw Sir John
Prostrate upon the floor.

'What now, old friend, unhappy Jack,
A sad loss you would be,
If I had really doted on
All that frivolity.

'You are the fattest deer to die
In battle here today,
But not the dearest that's for sure,
And I am bound to say...

'That it is quite amazing
That though you've suffered strife,
Your mountain of gross flesh could not
Retain a little life.'

And then without a backward glance
He slowly walked away;
Poor Falstaff, lying in the mud
Was lost for words to say.

But then he jumped onto his feet.
He said, 'Your pardon, lord.'
And, stabbing the dead Hotspur
With his sharp, trusty sword...

He slung the lifeless body
Across his ample back.
He carried Harry Hotspur's corpse
As if it were a sack.

But now approaching rapidly
Comes Prince Hal back again.
And straightaway Sir John exclaimed,
'My prince, look – I have slain...

'The bold and mighty Hotspur.
I killed him in fair fight.
He came around the moment
That you were out of sight.'

Prince Hal replied how sad it was
That Hotspur had to die,
And thus without a further word
Accepted this great lie.

The royal forces won that day,
And Falstaff was allowed
To claim he'd killed young Hotspur;
King Henry was so proud...

Of his bold son, the Prince of Wales,
He said, 'One thing, I'll lay
There seems a chance Prince Hal will make
A worthy king one day!'

~ ~ ~

The battle scarce was over when
More troubles were in store;
Rebels pooled their forces
To fight the king once more.

Their leaders all want action,
They're tired of idle talk,
They're led by Earl Northumberland
And the bishop of great York.

Though Henry now laments the fact
Disorder rules his realm,
His nobles give him confidence
That with him at the helm...

They can defeat the rebels,
Peace will return once more,
And everyone will live within
The monarch's royal law.

The whole affair comes to a head
When two great armies meet.
Their leaders have a parley,
But Henry's leaders cheat.

The royal forces there are led
By his young son, Prince John,
Who is about to carry out
The most enormous con.

He sends the Earl of Westmoreland
To have a little talk
With an opposing leader,
The bishop who's from York.

The bishop has a serious list
Of grievances to make;
Complaints against King Henry, all
'Made for the people's sake.'

Westmoreland says breezily,
'These points I do accede,
So now we have no cause to fight –
There really is no need.

'Let's each dismiss our army,
Let's all call it a day;
I'll get our monarch, Henry,
To sign this list today.'

The rebels sent their men away,
They took his word on trust,
For they were sure that Henry would
Prove honest, fair and just.

But Henry's son, the young Prince John,
In acting for his dad,
Turned out to be a devious chap,
A cunning, lying lad.

For once the rebel forces,
Disbanded, then withdrew,
The prince, who'd kept his army whole,
Then swiftly told them to...

Prepare for battle once again;
Return thus to the fight,
And using all their power and strength,
Their bravery and might...

Attack and mow the rebels down,
And catch their leaders too;
It really was a treacherous
And rotten thing to do!

~ ~ ~

Meanwhile back in London
The king is very sick,
But he is glad to hear the news
Of Prince John's sneaky trick.

His kingdom is now safe, and he
No longer needs to fear,
But as he learns of this good news
His own demise draws near.

Retiring to his bed, he rests,
And while he's fast asleep,
Prince Hal creeps to his bedroom
To take a little peep.

He looks upon his father then
And he becomes quite sure
That Henry, King of England, now
Lives and breathes no more.

He sees his country's royal crown
Upon the pillow there;
He leans across his father
And picks it up with care.

He takes it from the bedchamber –
For this is not a crime;
He truly thinks his hour has come –
It is Prince Harry's time.

But the king is merely sleeping
And when he wakes he cries,
'Where is my crown, where has it gone?
Don't count on my demise.'

Prince Hal comes back into the room;
His father sees him there.
He said, 'It seems, young Harry,
You hunger for my chair.'

Prince Hal replied, 'I never thought
To hear you speak again.'
His father said, 'I stay too long,
I see you're keen to reign.'

The prince did everything he could
With passionate emotion,
To calm him and convince the king
Of his great devotion.

Then Henry said, 'Sit down, my son.
I have not long to live,
And there is some advice I wish
From my heart to give.'

He gave his son good counsel,
Hal hung on everything;
At last there seemed an even chance
He'd make a decent king.

King Henry said, 'Now take me to
My chamber – there I'll lie,
And there in that Jerusalem,
Will sad King Henry die.

'I'll die within my chamber;
Yes, this is now my aim,
The one known as Jerusalem –
That bears that noble name,

'For it was prophesied to me
A long, long time ago,
I would die in Jerusalem,
And thus I'll make it so.'

~ ~ ~

And so King Henry passed away –
A new king was acclaimed:
Henry the Fifth of England
Prince Hal was now proclaimed.

His coronation was arranged,
A truly great affair,
A chance for all the common folk
To cheer and shout and stare.

The glorious procession
Set forth through London town,
Towards Westminster Abbey
Where Hal would claim his crown.

And as the pageant made its way
A man stepped from the crowd;
He was enormous, fat and round,
His voice was very loud.

'God save the King, my dear sweet boy!'
It was no other than
Jack Falstaff – but the king replied,
'I know you not, old man.

'And do not now presume to think
I am as once before,
The prince of past years has now gone –
Resides in me no more.'

Jack Falstaff stood there all aghast;
Could not believe his ears.
He was downhearted, mortified
And very close to tears.

He thought, 'I will be sent for,
To see him privately.
My dear, sweet prince would never turn
His face away from me.'

But it would never happen,
For now good friends – alack –
Falstaff would see all in good time
There was no turning back.

For with this one firm gesture
Prince Hal had made it plain,
He'd put aside his foolish ways —
Now was his time to reign.

This was a transformation:
Prince Hal had been dispatched,
And in his place, Henry the Fifth,
The ruler, had been hatched!

He rode across the field of blood

HENRY THE FIFTH

As we have seen, the young Prince Hal,
A playboy through and through,
When he became the English king –
Completely changed his view.

When he was crowned Henry the Fifth
It really turned his head.
'This must be taken seriously,'
With gravity he said.

He turned his back on fooling
With Falstaff all the time;
He now thought all frivolity
Was tantamount to crime.

~ ~ ~

And so our story opens
With two clerics who discuss
A matter that could cause the Church
A monumental fuss.

They are Ely's noble bishop,
And Canterbury's too.
The subject of their discourse
Has put them in a stew.

They are concerned that Henry –
Like his father once before –
Is after grabbing papal lands,
Ignoring every law.

Ely's bishop thus exclaimed,
Borne down and quite bereft,
'If he takes all he has in mind
There will be nothing left.'

Canterbury then replied,
'If this comes to befall,
In truth it surely must be said
'Twould drink the cup and all.'

Ely sighed, 'Oh what a trial,
On this we must confer,
What in the world can we both do
So this does not occur?'

Then Canterbury up and said –
Hope etched across his face –
'The king is of such fair regard
And now so full of grace...

'That he will maybe prove to be
A good and noble king
And listen with a kindly ear
To all the pleas we bring.

'For though he was a tearaway
When he was but a lad,
And though his every action caused
Distress to his poor dad...

'Once his father – the old king –
Was dead and breathed no more,
At once his wildness seemed to die;
It flew right out the door.

'His total reformation
Came on him like a flood,
And in the twinkling of an eye
He showed his royal blood.'

Ely mused, 'The strawberry grows
Beneath the stinging nettle,
So kings grow best with baser fruit
Before they show their mettle.'

Canterbury nodded then;
He said, 'All is not lost,
For I will make the king a gift
At some enormous cost.

'I'll offer him a goodly sum
To put him in our debt.
It is the largest pile of cash
The Church has given yet.

'You must believe me when I say,
It is a large advance,
And it is given with regard
To matters touching France.

'But more of that anon – for we
Must now be on our way,
Because the French ambassador
Craves audience today.

'He's come to see King Henry,
And so we'll shortly find
What he has come here to discuss;
What he's got on his mind.

'So with no hesitation,
And no more delay
Let's go unto the court to hear
All that he's got to say.'

~ ~ ~

King Henry sits amid his court,
Then Canterbury comes in.
The king is pleased to see the priest
And says with winning grin...

'I wish to ask advice of you,
For France is now my aim:
May I in rightful conscience make
Upon that land a claim...

'To take the French throne for myself?
I think it should be mine.
I beg you, good archbishop,
How does your will incline?'

Well, Canterbury then began –
And how the man could talk!
From giving an opinion
He'd never, ever baulk.

The priest went on and on until,
At last he said, 'It's true –
By right the royal throne of France
My lord, belongs to you.

'It's clear to any legal mind,
Your claim is justly made,
And gives the right for English might,
To go there and invade.

'And so, my good and gracious king,
The clergy give to you
More money than we have before
To do what you must do.'

Of course the wily cleric gave
This money with one hand,
In hope the other would hang on
To all the Church's land.

Henry's nobles there approved;
They thought it quite a plan.
They'd conquer France or each would die
A noble Englishman.

Henry was well pleased and said,
'We are within the law,
And once we've conquered France's lands
We'll win their minds, I'm sure...

'Or break them all in pieces –
So summon here to me
The French ambassador right now.
I'm eager thus to see...

'What messages he brings to court;
Let's hear him speak, I pray.
What is the news he would impart
To all of us today?'

The ambassador was summoned
And when he came he brought
A message from the Dauphin –
The heir to France's court.

Then once he had delivered
The Dauphin's salutation,
He carried on to speak about
Young Henry's reputation...

Of how he was so frivolous –
Of his unlucky falls –
And then he offered him a gift
Of sixteen tennis balls!

This was of course an insult,
A taunt to Henry's pride;
It made the point quite clearly
And mockingly implied...

That Henry should confine himself
To playing boyish games.
It was a rather subtle way
Of calling Henry names.

And its intended message –
Without a doubt, for sure –
The king should leave the craft of state
And weighty things like war...

To grown-up men and take himself
To youthful games again.
The king replied – and angrily;
He made his feelings plain.

He said, 'The Dauphin's action seems
Designed to make things worsen,
For it insults our national pride,
Likewise my royal person.

'So all that follows now will be
The Dauphin's fault alone,
For I am quite determined
To take his father's throne.'

He vowed that he was certain
He acted by God's laws.
He cried, 'The King of England comes!
Mine is a rightful cause.

'So forward into battle all,
Where we will take our chance,
We have no other thought except
The thought of winning France!'

~ ~ ~

So preparations start for war;
There's fever in the air,
But Henry hears a rumour
That he should now beware.

For he has learnt that three close earls,
Cambridge, Scroop and Grey
Are traitors to the crown and now
Are in the Dauphin's pay.

They plan to murder ruthlessly
Henry – their king and lord.
Apparently the three of them
Are all of one accord.

The king is in Southampton
To gather forces there;
And these three earls have been enticed
Right into Henry's lair.

They're unaware the noble king
Knows of their treachery;
They think their reputations are
Just what they used to be.

So Henry starts to play his game:
He asks Earl Scroop, 'What chance,
That we will be victorious
Against the might of France?'

'There is no doubt we shall succeed,'
Scroop says with utmost guile.
'And led by such a king as you,'
Grey says with slimy smile.

'Never was a king more loved
Or feared,' Earl Cambridge cried.
King Henry hearing these false words,
Just raised his eyes and sighed.

He took out three commissions
And handed them around.
The three earls grabbed the manuscripts
And read without a sound.

They thought these were their orders
For the impending war,
But each turned deathly pale to read
The words that he now saw.

They held their own death warrants,
Which clearly showed the reason
Why they were charged with treachery;
With villainous high treason.

Henry called them traitors.
'My downfall was your goal;
But you, Lord Scroop, have hurt me most –
You knew my very soul.'

They all admitted there and then
What traitors they had been,
What low and lying scoundrels –
The worst the court had seen.

The three all begged for mercy
But it was not to be.
Henry said, 'You've grieved me so
With your treachery.

'And yet I say that for myself,
I seek no great revenge,
But for betraying England's realm,
That crime I must avenge.

'So, you shameless wretches, go
To pay for this offence.
Go to your deaths – God help you all.
Soldiers, bear them hence.'

Boldly then King Henry said,
'The signs of war advance,
And I'll not be the English king
If not the King of France!'

~ ~ ~

We must take a detour now,
Back to old London town,
To where the king once played around
Before he wore the crown.

The Boar's Head tavern is the place
To which we must repair,
And, if you've read Henry the Fourth,
You'll know some people there.

They're Henry's former drinking pals
Who're also off to war;
Then worthy Mistress Quickly
Comes rushing through the door.

'Come to Sir John and hurry now,'
The hostess loudly cried.
'Come with all haste, I beg you,
Come now to his side.

'For he is racked with fever;
It's awful to behold.
He may not have that long to live –
At least that's what I'm told.'

Of course she spoke of Falstaff,
The king's old friend in fun;
That dear old fellow whom the king
Now sadly chose to shun.

Nym spoke tersely at her words,
'Aye, since the king departed,
Poor old Jack has been bereft,
Depressed and so downhearted.'

Pistol claimed, 'Oh yes, it's so.
Jack Falstaff never thought
His friendship with King Henry
Would one day count for naught.'

And then a little later on,
Sad news arrived indeed:
That Jack would never hunger for,
Would never ever need...

Another glass of wine, nor yet
Another harlot's bed,
Because in truth, Jack Falstaff
Was well and truly dead!

~ ~ ~

Meanwhile as Henry plans for war,
And that and that alone,
He still sends envoys off to France
To try to claim their throne.

Charles the Sixth, the King of France,
Hears all they have to say.
He listens to them grudgingly –
But there is just no way...

That he will merely step aside –
Let Henry have his realm.
He is determined and resolved
To stay right at the helm.

An envoy called Lord Exeter,
Makes Henry's feelings plain:
'All France belongs to England's king –
Her hills, her dales, the Seine!

'If Charles resists King Henry's claim,'
Lord Exeter then said,
'Then he, King Charles, must take the blame
For those who end up dead.

'France will be responsible
For everyone who dies,
For plaintive tears of widows and
For orphans' piteous cries...

'For all the tragic loss of life,
For all the blood and gore,
For husbands, fathers, brothers,
Who'll lose their lives in war.'

The king's son scowled and boldly said,
'Let Henry do his worst,
But tell him that he'll have to fight
With me, the Dauphin, first.'

Said Exeter, 'King Henry,
Whatever else befalls,
Will make quite sure he pays you back
For sending tennis balls!'

And so the scene was thus played out:
There'd be no more charades –
The time for talking was now through,
And war was on the cards!

~ ~ ~

The French and English kings both found
That neither could concur,
So Henry gave the word to sail:
'We head now for Harfleur.'

And once the mighty fleet arrived
They struggled to extort
A swift and speedy victory
From France's coastal port.

But this result, King Henry found,
Was sadly not to be.
Harfleur's courageous governor
Said, 'You don't frighten me.'

He closed the town's enormous gate –
Made ready for a siege;
A courtier said to Henry,
'This could take time, my liege.'

Henry nodded wearily –
Gave orders to surround
The now doomed port and told them all
To fight and hold their ground.

The siege went on for quite a while,
Until one fateful day
The king declared, 'I've had enough,
I'm going to have my way.'

So he approached the mighty gate –
He hailed the besieged town,
And from the mighty walls above
The citizens looked down.

The governor was there as well,
High up on the walls,
Then Henry called, 'Surrender now
Or take what fate befalls.

'For if you don't give up right now
It will be worse for you,
For I'll no longer guarantee
Just what my soldiers do.

'But if you open up the gate
I'll hold my soldiers back.
Your wives and children will be safe,
I'll spare them from attack.

'But if you still defy my wrath
And stubbornly persist,
If kindly acts of mercy you
Then gracelessly resist...

'I cannot guarantee my men
Will act with due restraint;
When finally we take your town –
They will not show constraint.

'Be sensible, surrender now,
Don't get my men annoyed;
And then all senseless bloodshed
We hopefully can avoid.'

The governor was not a fool
And he was most afraid:
He knew that there was little chance
His king would send them aid.

For he'd had word from France's court
They couldn't send relief,
And so the good man shouted down,
'It's now my firm belief...

'I have no choice, I have to yield
Before it is too late.'
And straightaway he gave the word
To open up the gate.

And thus the siege was over –
But what a price to pay!
For Henry's troops were tired out
And, it is true to say...

They had been very short of food –
Disease had struck some down;
No doubt they suffered heavily
When they besieged that town.

And winter was approaching –
So though the siege was won,
Disease and lack of sustenance
Had Henry on the run.

He knew he must retreat and come
To France again, next year.
He said, 'There'll be no fighting
For the present here, I fear.'

And so they set their weary way
For Calais, thus to go
Across the sea to England.
They'd not reckoned on their foe.

For the French were of a mind
That they would never yield.
And so they gathered forces
And took then to the field.

They pushed the English eastwards
And placed their armies might
'Twixt Henry's troops and Calais
Thus forcing him to fight.

Henry had nowhere to hide,
He had nowhere to run,
The French outnumbered Henry's force
Something like five to one.

It all looked most uncertain,
The odds were long indeed,
But Henry was determined
His forces would succeed…

And beat the French into the ground.
'We'll stand and fight,' he said,
'And we won't give an inch until
Our last brave man is dead.'

And that, of course, is where they stood,
And that is where they fought,
Upon the spot that's known by all,
Right there at Agincourt!

~ ~ ~

The sight before the battle,
The night before the fray
Was something those upon the scene
Recalled to their last day.

The air is filled with whispers,
They make a humming sound,
And in the French and English camps
A hundred fires abound.

And through the soft and velvet night
As many soldiers pray,
They hear the nervous whinnying
Of horses as they neigh.

And busy hammers work right through
That long and dreadful night,
Driving rivets into steel
To seal the armour tight.

The French are very confident
The battle will be theirs.
The English – weary and worn out –
Are quite borne down with cares.

But through the ranks of Englishmen
There walks the king awhile;
He bids his men, 'Good morrow,'
And gives a modest smile.

He calls them, 'Brother. Countrymen' –
His warm way has no end –
And as he makes his cheery way
He even calls them 'Friend.'

He walks with kingly manner
And on his royal face
There shows no sign of nervousness,
No, not the slightest trace.

His kind and cheerful majesty
Gives courage to the meek,
And even cowards, when he stops,
Cease thinking things look bleak.

He sheds a warmth just like the sun,
His presence thaws cold fear,
And everyone feels bold and brave
When royal Harry's near.

~ ~ ~

And so the day of battle dawns.
Asks Gloucester, 'Where's the king?'
Bedford replies, 'He views the troops –
It is the proper thing.'

'The French have sixty thousand men,'
Westmoreland glumly said.
'That's five to one,' sighed Exeter,
'And our men are half dead.'

Then King Henry joins his dukes
And hears Westmoreland say,
'Think of those not working
In England's realm today.

'If we had but a thousand here,
Fighting by our side,
We'd stand a chance of taking
Those Frenchmen for a ride.'

Calmly Henry answered him,
And with a little sigh;
He said, 'Not so, dear Westmoreland,
For if we are to die...

'It's best for all in England
That those who fall right here,
Should be as few as possible,
So please be of good cheer.

'And if our fate is that we live,
Then as we are so few,
A greater share of honour
Will thus become our due.

'Today we call St Crispin's Day –
I tell you, every year
That those who live will ever more
Regard this day as dear.

'And those who to old age survive
With pride will fondly say,
"Tomorrow is a special time
For it's St Crispin's Day"

'And they'll recount all that they did
When here upon this ground,
And as they speak their hallowed words
No-one will make a sound.

'The stories that their tongues relate
Will have a special ring –
Of Bedford and Lord Westmoreland,
Of Gloucester and the king.

'Each man will teach his son this tale,
Each year to be unfurled,
And it will be recalled until
The ending of the world.

'For we, this band of brothers,
We few, we happy few,
Will always be remembered
For what we are to do.

'And every man who sheds his blood
With me upon this day,
Will always be my brother
And he can always say...

'However humble was his birth –
Because he fought with me –
His actions here have earned their place
In England's history.

'And gentlemen who're now abed
In England's pleasant land
Will feel accursed they were not here
To give a helping hand.

'And when our men speak of this day
With honour and with pride,
Those absent will regret the fact
They weren't here by our side.

'They'll hold their manhood's cheaply,
As well indeed they may,
When any speaks who fought with us
Upon St Crispin's Day.'

~ ~ ~

And then the battle started,
A bloody, tangled fray,
And several times the cavalry
Of France did charge that day.

English bowmen stood behind
Stakes hammered in the ground,
And every time the French attacked
The English turned them round.

Arrows fell like hailstones on
The French troops underneath;
There didn't seem to be a spot
The French could find relief.

They floundered in a sea of mud
Brought on by autumn rain;
The English took advantage then
And pressed their hard-fought gain,

Till finally the French declared,
'The day is yours – you win!'
They asked if they could take their dead –
Collect their fallen kin.

There were ten thousand dead in all,
So many Frenchmen lost,
The Dauphin and the King of France
Could only count the cost.

The English army lost but few
In this great victory.
So Henry knelt in prayer and said,
'Thank God for aiding me.'

He rode across the field of blood,
Across the awful mess
Of injured soldiers, dying men,
Of mayhem and distress;

Of horses crippled in the mud,
Men beaten in the fray,
Of wounded men who still would live
To fight another day.

The king was moved and very sad
By everything he saw,
And yet he knew this was the price
Of fighting any war.

~ ~ ~

Henry left a force in France,
Then headed for the coast –
For Calais – then to England where
He was the nation's toast.

In London town, wherein he rode
In triumph through the streets,
The populace went crazy when
They heard of his great feats.

He was about as popular
As any king has been,
As loved and honoured and adored
As any monarch seen.

But in a little while the king
Returned to France again,
To make a peace and to agree
That now in France he'd reign.

A meeting was at once convened –
The King of France was there,
With his queen, and daughter too,
Sweet Katharine, so fair.

The Duke of Burgundy begins
To plead a dismal case –
He says that their beloved France
Now wears a sorry face.

'All our hedges lie untrimmed,
The grapes that make our wine
Remain neglected and unpicked;
They die upon the vine.

'Our fallow fields are in a mess,
All weeds and overgrown,
The meadows where sweet clover blew
Are left to grow unmown.

'But this is not the only thing,
As you will soon discern:
Our children now have no desire
To study or to learn.

'War is their only study now –
They swear and wear stern looks;
They show no interest at all
In reading from their books.

'And so, King Henry, I implore,
When will this suffering cease?
Why can't you banish all this strife
And give us gentle peace?'

The king replied with measured tone,
'If peace is your desire,
I beg you then agree my terms –
That's all that I require.'

The King of France then intervened.
He said, 'Give me a chance,
To read these terms again because
I gave them but a glance.'

As Charles and all his courtiers left,
The king said, 'If I may,
I beg your daughter, Katharine,
Should be allowed to stay.'

Fair Katharine remained behind
And as they closed the doors,
King Henry said, 'How can I, Kate,
Deserve a heart like yours?'

Kate spoke but little English,
So Henry tried his best
To make her understand his love
Was real and not a jest.

Finally she said to him
With many a nervous glance,
'Is it possible that I
Could love a foe of France?'

The king responded in a flash;
He said, 'I am no foe,
For I love France as much as you –
This I would have you know.

'I love your country far too much;
I want her to be mine.
When she is mine and I am yours
Our wishes will entwine.

'France will be yours – you'll be my wife,
So will you love me, Kate?'
Poor Henry had now worked himself
Into a nervous state.

'I will if my dear father
Agrees that I can wed.'
'Oh, he'll do that, without a doubt,'
King Henry boldly said.

And then the King of France returned
With Isabel, his queen,
And Burgundy and other lords
Arrived upon the scene.

Henry said with confidence,
'King Charles, upon my life,
I find that I can scarcely wait
For Kate to be my wife.'

King Charles replied in modest tone,
'If it so pleases you,
Then I don't have a problem
With what you wish to do.'

And then he said, 'I have agreed
To all the terms laid down.'
And in that moment Henry knew
He'd gained the French king's crown.

King Charles said, 'Take my daughter,
For you have truly won,
And give me children by her;
Give me heirs, my son.

'And let this stop all warring –
Let this now be the chance,
To bring a true alliance
'Twixt England and fair France.'

Henry took sweet Katharine's hand –
For he was very keen.
He said, 'Now all bear witness –
I kiss my sovereign queen.'

And then a trumpet call rang out,
And brave King Henry said,
'France and England will be joined
When Kate and I are wed.'

~ ~ ~

Sadly, Henry didn't have
Too long to be alive;
He was dead and buried by
The age of thirty-five.

He left a son, a puny child,
A helpless little thing.
He succeeded Henry as
Both France and England's king.

He became Henry the Sixth,
Theme of another play –
But that's a whole new story
To hear some other day.

*Then with a treacherous, fatal thrust
He takes King Henry's life*

HENRY THE SIXTH
Parts I, II & III

Henry the Fifth has sadly died,
His funeral's taking place,
And there is grief and sadness
On everybody's face.

For this king was dearly loved
While he had been alive,
And now to think he'd passed away
When only thirty-five.

It was the very saddest thing –
All stood before the Cross
In great Westminster Abbey
To mourn their grievous loss.

The Duke of Bedford then proclaimed,
'This king was just so strong,
And noble, good and virtuous –
Too famous to live long.

'And England never lost a king,
The country ne'er gave birth,
To monarch quite so dearly loved –
A king of so much worth.'

But as this gracious noble speaks
Of everything he feels,
A messenger comes rushing in;
Before the duke he kneels;

And then he gets onto his feet,
The dukes remain there seated;
He says, 'An English force in France
Is cruelly defeated.

'Talbot our brave commander,
Has lost the battle, so
He's now a prisoner of the French,
And also you should know...

'The Earl of Salisbury's now besieged
At Orleans, by mischance,
And finally the Dauphin, Charles,
Is crowned the King of France.'

The Duke of Bedford speaks out first.
'I'll not have this,' he cried.
'I'm going off to France right now,
Defeat, I'll not abide.'

The Duke of Gloucester spoke out too.
'I want to say one thing:
Henry the Fifth's small, infant boy
Must now be made our king.'

~ ~ ~

Meanwhile in France, Charles, now the king
Has made another raid
On Orleans – but fails again;
And then he meets a maid!

His cousin Bastard says to him,
'Although things look so dark,
I think I have the remedy –
Her name is Joan of Arc.

'And so although your face looks sad,
For discord rules our land,
I say my lord, be not dismayed
For succour is at hand.

'For here I bring this holy maid,
And though I risk derision,
I'm here to tell you that's she's had
The most amazing vision.

'It has come down from heaven above
While she was in a trance,
And she's been told that she will drive
The English out of France.'

And so Charles said, 'Go call her in,
For I could use some aid.'
Bastard left and soon returned
Accompanied by the maid.

Now Joan was not the type to hide
Her light beneath a bush;
To get whatever she desired
She'd always shove and push.

She told the Dauphin, now the king,
'I am the one you need
To send the English packing;
My sovereign lord – take heed.

'Let me lead the army;
I promise then you'll find
That you will quickly be released
From this awful bind.

'For I have seen a vision
From heaven, so I know
That I have been selected
To very boldly go...

'And save Orleans for the French,
And you must have no doubt
It is my fate – now Henry's dead –
To drive the English out.'

Well Charles was very sceptical,
For she was but a maid,
But he was in a rotten fix
And very much afraid...

The English would defeat him;
He'd grasp at any straw
For France to be victorious
In this horrendous war.

He said, 'I am astounded
With all you've had to say,
About this wondrous vision
You've shared with us today.

'But I say to be convinced –
To see what you can do –
I must in single combat
Now cross my sword with you.

'And if you vanquish me, I will
Believe your every word.'
Joan of Arc looked back at him
Quite calm and undeterred.

She chose her words most carefully,
'I am prepared, my lord,
To fight to prove my words are true –
See here my keen-edged sword.'

Charles replied, 'I swear to God
No woman do I fear.'
And then he drew his sword and said,
'Now everyone, stand clear.'

So they crossed swords and Joan of Arc
Said, 'This I'll do or die,
For while I live, I say in truth –
From no man will I fly.'

They fought until the king declared,
'A moment, stay thy hand.
You fight just like an Amazon
From some far, foreign land.'

The maid replied, 'I hope my king
You think me not a freak,
It is Christ's mother makes me strong;
Without her I'd be weak.'

The king replied – all business now –
'Whoe'er it is helps thee,
I little care, for I tell you,
'Tis you who must help me!'

And so a deal was quickly struck,
Joan said she would dispense
A thrashing to the English – then
Drive all the king's foes hence.

And she did all she promised, for
With sword and mace and lance,
She liberated Orleans town
And won it back for France.

King Charles was mightily impressed.
'She is God's chosen one.'
He said, ''Tis Joan, not we, by whom
This day is surely won.'

But soon his pleasure turns to ire;
The English then attack,
And with great skill and bravery
Win Orleans right back!

~ ~ ~

Meanwhile back in England
The earls are in dispute,
And squabbling over England's crown
Is at the quarrel's root.

Two factions now are forming;
There is much fighting talk
From earls who are of Lancaster
And those who are of York.

The Duke of York puts out his hand
And picks a sweet white rose;
He gazes at it longingly,
Then holds it to his nose.

'This rose shall be the symbol of
Our royal quest,' he said.
Warwick and Vernon copy him,
But others there pick red.

For Somerset and Suffolk,
With eagerness then chose
For Henry's house of Lancaster,
A glowing crimson rose.

And so as all these different earls
Placed flowers to their noses,
Their actions gave the title to
The sad Wars of the Roses...

In which these two great houses
Contested for the throne;
Each was intent and quite resolved
To have it for their own.

And then against this background
Of ominous unrest,
Gloucester, the king's Protector, said,
'We're lucky, we've been blest...

'With one who is a noble lad
To be our monarch – so
We'll travel now to Paris,
And there with pomp and show...

'We'll crown this worthy little lad;
Henry the Sixth, he'll be.'
And so without delay the court
Set out across the sea...

To crown this little boy the king
Of noble France's realm.
He'd be the ruler of two states,
At France *and* England's helm.

For this was way back in the days
When English kings still claimed
Jurisdiction over France,
When monarchs were thus named...

As King of France – and England too.
And so they planned with joy
A coronation for a king –
Though still a little boy.

~ ~ ~

The coronation over,
Attention now has turned
To fierce fighting with the French
Whose indignation burned.

Talbot, who has now been freed,
(A ransom has been paid),
Fights the French outside Bordeaux,
And asks to have more aid.

His forces are outnumbered,
He doesn't stand a chance;
Without more help there is no doubt
A win will go to France.

Alas, no further troops are sent
And Talbot, with his son,
Fight with their men until they see
The French have truly won.

But Talbot's son, the brave young John
Refused to run away.
He said, 'I am resolved, my lord,
That right here will I stay.

'For if I turn upon my tail
Before this fight is done,
I would be shamed for evermore
And not be Talbot's son.

'And so dear father, this I say,
I would much rather die,
Than leave the field with downcast head
And like a coward fly.'

Lord Talbot looked upon his son
And with a father's pride
He said, 'If you intend to stay,
Then I'll fight by your side.'

And so the father and the son,
Upon that dreadful day,
Took up their swords again to fight
Within that tangled fray.

They lost sight of each other, then
Lord Talbot took a wound;
Willing hands held him aloft,
They'd caught him as he swooned.

They laid him on the ground to rest,
And then some soldiers came;
They held a body steeped in blood –
They called John Talbot's name.

'Twas clear the person that they laid
Upon that blood-soaked sward
Was none other, than the son
Of the dying lord.

And as he lay there close to death,
His heart ached for his son,
He thought how awful fighting was,
Whichever side there won.

And then Lord Talbot realised
On seeing the blood shed,
That his adored, courageous boy –
His dear son, John – was dead.

'Oh, my lost boy,' he gasped aloud.
'Please lay him by my side
So I can wrap him in my arms.'
Oh, how Lord Talbot cried.

He shook with sheer emotion,
He said, 'Now all I crave
Is that my ancient arms can be
Poor young John Talbot's grave.'

They set the boy with care within
Lord Talbot's outstretched arm.
He wrapped his other round his son,
As if to stave off harm...

In just the way he'd done before,
So many years ago
When John had been a little boy,
Eyes bright and face aglow.

Lord Talbot said no further words,
There was no more to say,
And holding his beloved son
The sad lord passed away.

~ ~ ~

Though England was defeated,
It didn't take too long
For forces to regather
To right what they thought wrong.

And after further fighting
The English made their mark,
They captured as their prisoner
The French maid – Joan of Arc.

They took her to the English camp,
She begged them for her life,
But hatred for the wretched maid
By then was running rife.

The Duke of York insulted her,
And though she was so young –
He called her hag and other things
And told her, 'Hold your tongue!'

But Joan replied and bravely;
She said, 'Do not make haste,
For I have lived a decent life,
Blameless, good and chaste.'

But York would hear no word of it,
He wanted retribution.
He cried, 'Enough, just take her out!
See to her execution.'

She was sentenced right away,
They told her then and there
They'd tie her to a stake – she'd burn
In Rouen's market square.

Then Warwick, he of kindly heart,
Said, 'I would like to make
A merciful attempt to ease
Her torture at the stake.

'Spare no faggots for the fire,
Let there be wood enough
So that her pain and suffering
Is short and not too tough.'

Joan cried out, and desperately –
Her words tore some apart –
'Will nothing have effect upon
Your unrelenting heart?

'For I am now with child,' she said.
Don't send it to its doom;
This little baby lives right now –
A child within my womb.'

But York cried out, 'Good heavens!
The holy maid with child!
It could be, the Dauphin has
Himself this lass defiled.

'But it will make no difference,
And it is all a lie;
Your pleadings will not save you
For you are doomed to die.'

'Then lead me hence,' the maid replied,
'For I will plead no more.'
They took her by each arm and led
The poor girl through the door;

And as she left she laid a curse
With her last living breath:
'I hope your country suffers
The gloomy shades of death.

'And may great mischief and despair
Within your land reside,
And drive you to the breaking point
And then to suicide.'

York answered her, 'Now be consumed,
And as you thus expire,
Know you are nothing, Joan of Arc,
So go now to the fire.

'For you are surely cursed and doomed
By some dread, awful spell,
And so begone – thou foul accursed
Minister of hell.'

And so they took her out to die;
They tied her to a stake,
And there they burned the maid to death –
But she left in her wake...

A story that has stirred the souls
Of men through history;
Of how, though but a mere girl,
She tried to set France free.

~ ~ ~

Shortly after these events
The French king said, 'All right,
Let's call a truce and let's agree
We will no longer fight.'

Henry made him Viceroy,
So everything was fine;
Their efforts for the present,
The pair would now combine.

Meanwhile the Earl of Suffolk
Stood up and archly said,
'I think our new King Henry
Should now be getting wed.

'And though he still is very young
I think that this young man
Should marry someone right away –
In fact, I have a plan.'

He said that Margaret of Anjou
Would be the one for him.
'She's very pretty in the face
And very lithe of limb.'

What he didn't say of course,
That sneaky, devious Earl,
Was that *he'd* had a hushed affair
With this fair, comely girl.

'If I can set this up,' he thought,
'It could be good for me.'
So he was pleased when Henry said
He'd readily agree.

He'd gladly wed the lady,
She really looked first-rate,
She'd make a lovely wife and queen,
She'd make an ideal mate.

The earl was quietly overjoyed
To see this union flower;
He thought through young, sweet Margaret
He'd exercise all power.

'I'll rule young Margaret and the king
And thus control the realm;
Though no-one else will realise,
I shall be at the helm.

'The destiny of England
I'll hold – within my hand,
And it will be good Suffolk
Who rules this troubled land!'

~ ~ ~

So Suffolk travelled then to France,
He went without ado,
Just with the aim of bringing back
Young Margaret of Anjou.

He settled terms with her pleased dad
But on arriving back,
He found expressions on some dukes
That looked extremely black.

They do not like what he's agreed
To cede to Margaret's dad;
Gloucester, Warwick, York as well,
All think the deal is bad.

For he has given at a stroke
Maine and Anjou too –
Back to France – and all he's got
Is Margaret of Anjou.

Henry though is happy,
For he likes the look
Of the girl he's now to wed –
She's quite a lass to hook.

But he'd have been upset and hurt,
A most unhappy king,
If he'd had knowledge of the fact
That Suffolk's sneaky fling...

Was still alive and carrying on,
For Suffolk was intent
On keeping Margaret on a string –
On this he was hell-bent.

But anyway, the king is pleased
With all that's now in place;
He doesn't care he's given lands
When he sees Margaret's face.

The Duke of York is horrified,
The Earl of Warwick too;
They do not like the deal one bit,
They hate it through and through.

Even the Duke of Gloucester,
Who's Protector to the king,
Thinks Suffolk has now gone and done
A really stupid thing.

And yet, despite his senior role,
Gloucester has much to fear;
The best advice for him is this;
'Be sure to watch your rear.'

For many hate the mighty duke
As he is wont to boast
That he is closest to the king
Just through his special post.

And there's the chance that he could be
The victim of attack.
Yes Gloucester, if he's got good sense,
Should really watch his back.

He has another problem too
That causes him some strife,
And that's his lady duchess,
Sly Eleanor – his wife.

She is a rather silly sort
For she's inclined to preen,
And she informed him one fine day,
'I fancy being queen.'

This sort of thing was typical
For it must now be said
That some at court had oft remarked
She had a swollen head.

And Margaret, now queen, would cry
In anger, 'Look at her
Done up in her finery
And wearing all that fur.

'Whoever does she thing she is?'
And then the queen would snort,
'She acts just like an empress
The way she comes to court.

'And strangers here, in truth do think,
When they at first have seen
Old Gloucester's daft, ambitious wife
That she's in fact the queen.'

Now Gloucester often chided
His wife for her grand way,
But she would just ignore the words
The harassed duke would say.

For just her own vain, silly thoughts
Careered around her head,
And she took no account at all
Of what her husband said.

And so this was the state of things
When Henry said one day,
'Order Gloucester here at once,
Summon the duke, I pray.'

The king was in St Albans
And Gloucester hurried there.
As he left his wife called out,
'I'll see you soon – take care.'

And once he'd gone, she hurried off
To carry out a scheme
That was as crazy as the look
That in her eye did gleam.

For now she took herself to see
A witch within her den.
She said, 'I've come here to consult,
For you to tell me then...

All that the spirit does foretell,
So ask it now for me.
Will I become the queen one day?
What will the future be?'

And so the awful, ugly witch
Called up a spirit then,
Who said, 'I've got some news right here
Concerning two proud men.'

And then her weak, old croaking voice
Said with a little groan,
'The King of England, Henry
Will soon be overthrown.

'Also the Duke of Suffolk,
That mean and sneaky chap,
On water is now destined
To suffer a mishap.'

Eleanor gasped aloud at this
But ere she could say more,
There came a heavy pounding
Upon the witch's door.

Then York and Buckingham with guards
Came roughly bursting in,
And they told Eleanor with scorn
That what she did was sin.

And they arrested her and took
Her straight before the king,
Who shouted, 'You should really die
For this horrendous thing.

'Consulting with the witches is
The worst sin one can do.
The penalty for this is death,
And this I'm sure you knew.

'But as you are most nobly born
I'll just impose a ban.'
And so he banished her that day
Unto the Isle of Man.

He said, 'Before you go you'll walk
The streets of London town,
Where common folk can shout at you;
You'll wear a ragged crown.

'And this humiliation
Will entertain the crowd,
And make you cease for evermore
From being vain and proud.

'And as for you, Duke Gloucester,
I should really have you whipped,
But the title of Protector
Is from your shoulders stripped.

'And now I have no further wish
To look upon your face.'
So Gloucester left to contemplate
His mighty fall from grace.

~ ~ ~

Meanwhile the harassed Duke of York
Speaks with a furrowed frown
To Salisbury and to Warwick;
They're all in London town.

He said, 'By right, I should be king.'
He got into a lather.
'My family's rights were once usurped
By the king's grandfather.

'When Bolingbroke assumed the crown
He stole my family's throne,
For it belonged by ancient right
To us – and us alone.'

Warwick and Salisbury bent the knee
On hearing this bold talk.
'You are our rightful sovereign, sire,'
They tell the Duke of York.

York nods his head and slowly says,
'Yes, what you say is true,
But before I can be king
There's much for us to do.

'The white rose of the Yorkist cause
Will now defeat,' he said,
'The blood red rose of Lancaster,
When its false king is dead.'

But news then came of trouble –
In Ireland it occurred –
And in no time, the Duke of York
Received the royal word...

That he must travel there and quell
This latest discontent.
And so he quickly packed his bags
And that is where he went.

It was a timely act indeed –
Henry's command that day –
For at a stroke he'd got sly York
Quite safely out the way.

~ ~ ~

The king calls Gloucester back to him.
Alas, his only reason
Is so that Suffolk can arrest
The poor old duke for treason.

They led Gloucester from the room
And as he went he cried
To Henry and he warned the king,
'My lord, watch every side,

'For you have foes on every flank.
They're bent on evil ends.
My lord, remember what I say:
You don't have many friends.'

Queen Margaret says to Suffolk,
'I wish Duke Gloucester dead.
I'll only be relaxed for sure
When we've chopped off his head.'

She'd never liked the sad, old duke,
And now she thought, 'I may
Have my best chance to deal with him
And get him out the way.'

Her comment was enough to help
Set events in motion,
That were likely to then cause
A really great commotion.

For a little later on
Sly Suffolk came to say
The Duke of Gloucester had just now
Most sadly passed away.

King Henry turned quite white with shock;
He cursed and loudly swore,
And then he went into a swoon
And fell onto the floor.

Everyone was so amazed
To see him lying there;
It seemed King Henry found the news
A mite too hard to bear.

You see, he was kind-hearted,
Still had a soft spot for
Old Gloucester, even though the duke
Was close to him no more.

When he came round he hit the roof;
He turned on Suffolk then
And said in no uncertain terms
He was the worst of men.

He blamed him for Duke Gloucester's death,
But then the queen jumped in;
She said to blame poor Suffolk there
Was really a bit thin.

But now Earl Warwick enters.
'Gloucester's dead,' he said.
'I think the duke was strangled
As he lay on his bed.

'His face was black and full of blood,
His eyeballs further out
Than ever in his life they were –
Of this I have no doubt.'

Henry lost control and said,
'All these foul deeds must halt.
And Suffolk, I blame you for this:
His death is all your fault.

'And so I banish you for good.
Don't ever come back here.'
The queen on hearing this, broke down,
And said she felt quite queer.

She cried, 'Oh, gentle Henry,
Let me plead for Suffolk there,
He's always been so good to you
And shown you every care.'

The king replied with flashing eyes,
Red faced and all a-froth,
'I tell you, if you plead for him,
'Twill just increase my wrath.

'And Suffolk, I do swear to you,
Despite my pleading wife,
If in three days you're in my realm,
Why then you'll lose your life.

'For if we find your worthless hide
Still lurking in our land,
The world itself won't ransom you
From death by axeman's hand.'

Then he called, 'Come Warwick,
Good Warwick, come with me,
For I have matters of import
That I would share with thee.'

Now alone – the lovers there –
Earl Suffolk and the queen,
Created such a woeful sight –
A most distressing scene.

The queen cried, 'Let me take your hand
And cover it with tears.'
Suffolk took her in his arms
And tried to quell her fears.

She sighed, 'My lord, when you depart,
You take my life as well.
Where will you go? How will you fare?
Wherever will you dwell?'

Suffolk sighed, 'It matters not,
I really couldn't care,
For desolation rules supreme,
If you, my love, aren't there.'

And so they made their last farewells.
The queen said, 'Leave with me
Your loving heart, sweet Suffolk and
Take my true heart with thee.'

And thus the lovers said goodbye,
A scene of bitter woe.
Suffolk turned and simply said,
'And now my queen, I go.'

He left her there, bereft, alone,
And with no backward glance,
He headed off to banishment,
Across the sea to France.

~ ~ ~

So Suffolk left the court and went
From there to board a ship.
The last thing that he wanted
Was thus to make this trip.

But exile's what he's got in store,
King Henry's had enough
Of all his scheming, lying ways –
At last he's acting tough.

But on the way to his new life
Earl Suffolk gets a shock.
He's captured by some pirates and
His head is on a block.

They tell him he's about to die;
Suffolk's face turns white,
He says, 'It's quite impossible.
It really isn't right...

'That I should die by menial hands
Of vassals such as you;
You're too lowborn, contemptible,
For what you plan to do.

'A noble lord should be dispatched
By better folk, you know'
They laughed and said, 'We'll handle you
Like any other foe.'

And so they chopped his head right off,
Then – being very mean –
They wrapped it up and sent it as
A present to the queen.

And when the queen received it
She got into a flap.
She cried out loud and vowed revenge
And hugged it to her lap.

She gasped, 'Here may his sweet head lie.'
She looked down on his face.
'But where's his noble body which
I should now here embrace?'

King Henry scowled with fearsome glare –
'How now, my dear,' he said.
'Would you have mourned so much for me
If it were me there dead?'

The queen was quick to answer.
'If it were you – you'd see
That I would never, ever mourn,
For I would die 'twere thee.'

So we can see the queen was smart,
Artful and all knowing.
In an instant she worked out
The way the wind was blowing.

~ ~ ~

Now things begin to gather pace.
The Duke of York returns
From Ireland and within his heart
A great ambition burns.

While he's been absent, he's had friends
Who've caused a great revolt;
It's really shaken Henry up
And given him a jolt.

For York has been hard at it –
He's done his very best,
To get a chap who's called Jack Cade
To stir up great unrest.

Cade's led a strong rebellion,
He's marched on London town.
He had the fervent aim in mind
To bring King Henry down.

The Duke of Buckingham however,
Stopped him in his tracks,
And cut a deal to save the town
From any more attacks.

He pardoned everyone with Cade,
If they would leave his cause.
He said, 'We cannot settle this
By having civil wars.'

So they'd abandoned poor Jack Cade
And he had taken flight,
But then he had been caught and killed
While on the run one night.

So this is how the kingdom stood
When York came back again,
And he was still determined that
He'd end King Henry's reign.

For this was now his time, he thought.
He'd grab the English throne,
For Henry only had the crown
On just a short term loan.

And so he sends a false demand
That if the king arrests
The Duke of Somerset – that man
Whom he so much detests,

Well then, and only then, will he
Pull all his forces back.
Of course he hopes the king will say,
'Just do your worst – attack!'

He's marched his troops on London,
Confident he'll teach
The king respect and that the crown
Is now within his reach.

Buckingham rode to meet him,
And York said, 'If it's proved
That Somerset whom I detest
Is sacked and quite removed...

'Then and only then, I'll stop
This march on London town,
And if he's sacked, I'll pledge myself
To Henry and the crown.'

His demand is merely pretence,
He hopes the king will say,
'The Duke of York can do his worst,
He shall not have his way.'

For this will give him reason
To carry on the fight;
He'd used the Duke of Somerset
To make his cause look right.

When York is told that Somerset
Is now no longer free –
He has no option but to pledge
His total loyalty.

But then he hears from someone else
This claim is quite untrue.
Somerset, whom he detests –
The man he would undo...

Is walking round as free as air,
And so the duke then swore
That Henry's days were numbered.
He vowed, 'He'll reign no more.'

The armies then were both prepared
And battle lines were drawn.
They met outside St Albans,
Upon one early dawn.

King Henry's house of Lancaster
Opposed the Yorkists there,
To battle for the English throne;
To find out who would wear...

The crown of England. Who'd be king?
And so the fight began,
But it did not take long at all
Before the king's troops ran.

Henry fled to London,
And York, with great delight,
Said, 'What a massive victory!
We *did* put up a fight!

'But now we must proceed with haste
To good old London town,
And there kick Henry from the throne
And quickly claim the crown.'

~ ~ ~

The Duke of York is really sure
That this is now his hour,
And he takes steps right there and then
To seize all royal power.

But Henry soon comes on the scene,
And though things look quite bleak,
He acts as if he's still the king
And says, 'You've got a cheek.'

And then he really vents his wrath –
He really has a moan;
He says to York, 'You'd better get
Your eyes from off my throne.'

York wouldn't heed a word of this.
He said, 'You need to know
I am now England's rightful king,
For you have had your go.

'It's now my turn to rule this land –
Look at the mess you've made.'
With bold fine words, King Henry said,
Although a bit afraid...

'My title to the throne comes through
My dear old grandad who
Was just as noble in his birth
And worthier than you.

'Henry the Fourth, my grandpapa,
A man of great renown,
A decent and fair-minded man,
By conquest won the crown.'

But as he spoke, King Henry
Well knew he partly lied,
And turning from the Duke of York
He said as an aside...

'I know my title's somewhat weak
For grandad stole the throne,
But that's a long way in the past;
We'll leave all that alone.'

But York's insistence he be king
Knocks Henry right off track,
And his resolve and stubbornness
Begin at last to crack.

For what he then proposes takes
All present by surprise:
He says, 'I'll tell you what we'll do
By way of compromise.

'I'll remain the king, but when
I've shuffled from this life,
When I am dead and live no more,
When free of all this strife;

'When I've laid down my burden
And said goodbye to care,
Well I do then propose, good York,
That you become my heir.

'And all your sons that follow you
Should also claim the crown.'
On hearing this, Queen Margaret's face
Took on a fearsome frown.

'How can you give away your throne?'
The queen, distraught, bewails.
'How can you disinherit thus
Your son – the Prince of Wales?'

But the Duke of York agrees,
It seems to be the thing
To settle matters and it means
One day he will be king.

~ ~ ~

The Duke of York has made his way
To Sandal Castle, where
His sons tell him he must resort
To bloody, bold warfare.

'It is the only way,' they say.
And then they tell him why.
'For you must be the country's king
Or be prepared to die.

'You cannot wait around for years;
The crown is yours by right,
So father there is just one course —
We must now stand and fight.'

So war breaks out once more and now
The two great armies meet,
But after heavy fighting
York's forces all retreat.

The Duke of York is captured,
He's taken to the queen;
I think we know already that
She's pretty tough and mean.

She laughs at him and harshly hurls
Great insults at the duke,
But he was not the type to take
So vulgar a rebuke.

And though he was a prisoner
And at her mercy there,
He began to rage and fume,
To shout at her and swear.

Lord Clifford too, was with the queen,
And he had cause to hate
The Duke of York, for Clifford's dad
Had sadly met the fate...

Of early death, when he'd been killed
Upon St Albans field.
He'd fought against the Yorkists
And had refused to yield.

And so Lord Clifford blames the duke.
He thinks that he's just bad.
He holds him guilty for the loss
Of his beloved dad.

And then Lord Clifford and the queen
Both did an awful thing;
They leapt upon the duke and stabbed
This man who would be king.

The Duke of York died painfully,
He fell down with a thud,
And lay there on the floor within
A pool of his own blood.

The queen looked down at him and said
With monumental scorn,
'Take him to York and there behead
This traitor, vilely born,

'And put his head upon a stake
And let the people gawk
At this low creature rotting there;
This vulgar son of York.'

~ ~ ~

The news of York's demise is brought
To two of his dear boys.
Edward and Richard hear with pain
Of all the queen's foul ploys.

Of how she'd taunted their dear dad,
Of all that he'd been through;
And hearing this just made them vow
To gird their loins anew.

And then some more bad news arrives,
It tells of a defeat,
But says their other brother George,
Is still intent to beat...

King Henry and his forces;
And so he comes – this George –
With many troops from Burgundy,
And now is set to forge...

A path right through King Henry's force;
He's set on his endgame,
To bring King Henry down and then
Enforce the Yorkist claim.

~ ~ ~

Meanwhile in York the queen displays
The poor duke's severed head.
King Henry there was mortified –
'Oh awful deed!' he said.

But now York's sons have mobilised
Another army, so
They're set to have another try,
To have another go.

For they're determined that the Yorks
Will somehow gain the crown,
That Henry must receive at last
His overdue comedown.

And so another battle's fought,
This time the Yorkists win;
King Henry's forces all turn tail
And cry, 'We're giving in.'

So Henry too then fled the field
And as he did he said,
'I grieve to see these bodies here,
Sons, brothers, fathers – dead!'

And then he sees a boy bring in
His own dad whom he's killed,
And next a father brings his son
Whose blood he's also spilled.

And Henry there and then laments –
He's shaken to the core.
He hates relations fighting,
He loathes all civil war.

For it is so barbaric,
Families split in two;
It's really such a ghastly
And dreadful thing to do.

And so he turns his back and goes,
Leaves all the blood and gore,
And hopes that it will be the end
Of this infernal war.

~ ~ ~

As Henry left the field of blood
Lord Clifford was then found,
By Edward and young Richard
Lying wounded on the ground.

'So what have we got here?' they say.
'Well, this is quite a prize!'
But as they taunt Lord Clifford
The wounded man there dies.

However, they still curse at him,
Although the man is dead.
And then as one they say, 'For dad,
Let's cut off his foul head.'

So to avenge their father's death
They make Lord Clifford pay.
They take his severed head to York
And put it on display.

They then put plans in place to make
Edward, fair England's king.
Richard and George gain titles too
That have a noble ring.

George is the Duke of Clarence
And Richard there and then,
Is made the Duke of Gloucester –
He's quite the worst of men.

For now he ponders to himself,
'How can I get the throne?
How many must I tread upon
To make the crown my own?'

Alone he contemplated
The spot on which he stood,
And said, 'I feel I'm standing
Within a thorny wood...

'From which I now must free myself;
I really can't relax,
Till I have hewn my way from here
With sharp and bloody axe.

'And nobody shall block my path
For if they do, I'll strike,
And all will feel my awful wrath,
Brother and foe alike.

'For I will murder anyone
With ruthlessness and guile,
And I can do all this with ease
And murder while I smile.'

It soon became apparent then
That he'd do anything
To push all others from his path
In order to be king.

What a villain! And I'm sure
He's one of whom you've heard,
For in time this duke became
King Richard, England's third.

~ ~ ~

King Henry now is on the run,
He hides within a wood.
He's mumbling to himself and says,
'Margaret, my queen, is good,

'For she has gone to Paris
To ask King Lewis there
If he will send some help to me
And heed this poor king's prayer.'

But as he's talking to himself
Two gamekeepers are near.
They're tramping through the forest;
One says, 'What's that I hear?'

They spot the king in hiding
And when they see him there
They recognise him instantly –
They'd know him anywhere.

They grab him and arrest him,
Take him within the hour
Before his enemies, who then
Confine him in the Tower.

~ ~ ~

Edward meanwhile is intent,
Beginning his new life,
To find himself a partner –
A fine and wealthy wife.

His choice alights on Lady Grey.
His brothers tell him straight,
'She's not the person to be queen,
For you she's no fit mate.'

But Edward's mind is quite made up.
He says, 'I'm set to marry,
And I can tell you one and all
I don't intend to tarry.'

The Earl of Warwick, who has played
A loyal helping hand
In making Edward England's king,
Now makes his own bold stand.

He doesn't like the news at all
Of Edward's plan to wed.
'I'll now support King Henry;
I'm changing sides,' he said.

And then he reached agreement for
His daughter, Lady Anne,
To marry Henry's worthy son,
A fine upstanding man:

This was the valiant Prince of Wales,
And so without delay
The two young people eagerly
Agreed their wedding day.

Then Warwick led his army on
A bloody, great onslaught;
He overpowered King Edward's troops,
And Edward then was caught.

And after they had locked him up
The earl went straightaway
To free King Henry from the Tower –
He went that very day.

So Henry thus regained his throne,
Became the king once more;
And he rejoiced in being king
The way he had before.

But while he was rejoicing
Upon this change of luck,
Some news came in that left him
Amazed and quite dumbstruck.

For Richard, Duke of Gloucester had
Sprung Edward from his jail,
And they had both escaped to France;
King Henry went quite pale.

And, truthfully, he had good cause,
For in no time at all
Edward and Richard had returned
For yet another brawl.

They came with massive forces
And marched on London town,
Even more determined
To seize the English crown.

They captured Henry once again,
And stripped him of his power,
And once more ignominiously
They threw him in the Tower.

It all comes to a head quite soon
When two great armies meet,
Advancing on each other,
Each praying they'll defeat...

The other side with little loss.
They're both intent to win,
For neither side has any thought
Of ever giving in.

Queen Margaret leads King Henry's troops,
Set to defend his realm;
The other's led by Edward –
He rides there at the helm.

The armies clash on Tewkesbury field
And, after a great fight,
Edward's forces win the day;
Margaret's all take flight.

Queen Margaret is captured then;
The Prince of Wales is too.
Edward says to Wales, 'Good sir,
What shall we do with you?'

The Prince of Wales is young and brave;
He calls his captors names,
He mocks all Edwards 'fancy' plans,
Derides his regal claims.

'Lascivious Ed!' he calls him.
Richard – 'Misshapen Dick.'
He said, 'You and your brothers
Make me and my dad sick.'

The brothers wouldn't stand for this.
They said, 'Now watch your tongue.
We won't take cheeky talk like that
From someone who's so young.'

But the Prince of Wales was brash,
He let his insults fly,
So Edward and his brothers there
Decided he must die.

And thus without another word,
George – Richard – Edward too,
Leapt forward all declaring,
'We will now silence you.'

Right there before his mother
These three grim Yorkist males
All stabbed King Henry's much loved son;
They killed the Prince of Wales.

Then Richard, Duke of Gloucester
Right on that very hour,
Jumped on his horse and rode all night
To London and the Tower.

He made his way to Henry's cell,
Within those thick, grey walls.
It's there the final act of hate
'Twixt these two sides befalls.

Gloucester told the jailor, 'Go!
Leave us alone, good sir.
It is essential that you leave
For we must now confer.'

'So flies the restless shepherd
From the wolf,' King Henry cried.
'Suspicion haunts the guilty mind,'
The evil Gloucester sighed.

'You've come to kill me,' Henry breathed.
Richard of Gloucester said,
'You think I wish your swift demise,
Just like your son who's dead.'

Henry groaned as he dwelt on
His son, of so much worth.
He cried, 'An owl shrieked out upon
The moment of your birth.

'And dogs howled then – a tempest shook
The trees and pulled them down,
And ravens croaked on chimney pots
In every English town.

'For you were born with many teeth
And this did signify,
You came into the world to bite
And cause good folk to die.

'You are a foul, ungodly sight,'
King Henry spoke with scorn.
'Thousands will come to rue the day
This Yorkist cur was born.'

This insult Richard quite ignores
And swiftly draws his knife;
Then with a treacherous, fatal thrust
He takes King Henry's life.

As Henry drew his final breath
He sank onto one knee
And cried, 'O God, forgive my sins –
Gloucester, I pardon thee.'

Then he collapsed upon the floor:
Said Gloucester, with a sigh,
'King Henry and his son are gone
But now some more must die.

'For I would have the throne and so
Some kin must die as well.'
Without a doubt, this Yorkist lord
Was like a fiend from hell.

And with this act of murder
Our sorry tale now closes.
It drops the final curtain on
The sad Wars of the Roses.

For Edward now was free to rule;
He'd won through everything
And now became Edward the Fourth
To reign as England's king.

But if you wish to find out more
Of all that then occurred,
You'll have to read the story of
King Richard, England's third.

He lacks all royal charm

RICHARD THE THIRD

Our story opens gently
Within the royal court
Of Edward, King of England,
Who's quite a decent sort.

And standing to one side of him,
Observing everything,
Is Richard, Duke of Gloucester,
Who yearns to be the king.

Edward's his oldest brother
And, though not next in line,
Richard vowed, 'When Edward dies,
The throne – I'll make it mine!'

Before he can achieve this end,
Before this longed-for day,
There are some folk he'll have to stop
From getting in his way.

But for the moment let us watch
And see him standing there;
A menacing, black spider that
Has ventured from his lair.

He's talking to himself and if
We listen for a while
We'll get a true impression of
His most unpleasant style.

But before we hear him speak
Consider how he looks,
For he has been described this way
In many history books.

He has a threatening manner –
A sight to cause alarm;
His hair is black, his face is pale –
He lacks all royal charm.

And now he speaks and it is clear
He reeks of discontent,
He loathes himself, his dismal life,
The cards that he's been sent.

'We've taken off our armour
And now it's hanging up,
Just useless decorations while
We all carouse and sup.

'Instead of stern intentions
As we go off to war,
We all wear blithe expressions
And dance around the floor.

'Instead of mounting fearsome steeds,
Most plead a lover's suit,
Pursuing ladies to the sound
Of a seductive lute.

'But I'm not made for life at court
With its continual leisure,
I quite detest these wasted days,
I hate all idle pleasure.

'None of this appeals to me,'
Beneath his breath he swore;
'I'm weary of its dreariness –
I cannot stand much more.

'It doesn't suit my character –
So bleak, that when dogs spy
My huddled form along the street
They bark, yet know not why.

'But I have been so badly formed,
I am not made to be
Flirtatious with the ladies – no –
They are not drawn to me.

'And I'm not made to spend my time
Before a looking glass;
To thus admire myself this way
Would surely be a farce.

'So if as lover I can't act,
Or emulate his ways,
I'm resolved I'll prove a villain
In these forthcoming days.

'For I intend to gain the throne,
But ere that happy day,
I must get my other brother
Completely out the way.

'For I'm determined that the king
And Duke Clarence – our brother –
Shall both of them unite in hate,
The one against the other.

'To do this, I've informed the king
About a prophecy
Which says that someone with a name
That starts with letter G...

'Will conspire to take his children
From safe within his sight,
And murder them most awfully
Within the dead of night.

'My brother, Clarence, is called George,
With luck the king will think
That he's a mortal enemy
And throw him in the clink.

'But here comes brother Clarence now,
With such a scowling face!
Greetings brother – why this guard
That waits upon your grace?'

Clarence smiled to see him there,
He thought he was his friend.
Little did he realise
That Richard sought his end.

'The king hears prophecies,' he said,
'Heeds old wives' tales, it seems,
That say his heirs will all be killed –
He sees this in his dreams.

'The murderer's name begins with G,
And so within the hour
Of hearing this he made his plans
To throw me in the Tower.'

'Alack, my lord,' dark Richard said,
'I know you're not to blame.
It's just your sad misfortune that
George is your Christian name.

'But do not fear, I'll to the king,
Where I will plead for you.
I find this quite peculiar and
It's most distressing too.'

Clarence thanked his brother,
But as he went away,
Richard with a wicked sneer,
Had other words to say.

'Go tread the path, dear Clarence,
From which you'll not return,
You're simple, plain and trusting,
For you will never learn...

'That I love you so very much
That I will send your soul,
To heaven as a special gift:
Your death is now my goal.'

~ ~ ~

And then news came to Richard,
The king was sick and weak;
Richard, when he heard of this
Looked downcast, sad and bleak;

But this of course was just an act,
Deceitful, sly flim-flam;
He hoped the king would die and so
It was all but a sham.

Once on his own he archly said,
'With luck the king will die,
But not before he's acted on
My softly spoken lie.

'For Clarence must be heaven bound
Before the king quits life.
I'll to him now and feed his fears
And make them all run rife;

'And if my plan succeeds – well then
I think I'd only give
My trusting brother Clarence
Another day to live.

'Then once sad Clarence is quite dead,
Then God – take Edward too,
And leave me free to carry out
Those things I yearn to do.

'For then this world will be my own,
For me to bustle in;
But now I'll make all haste to set
My sights to quickly win...

'The hand of comely Lady Anne,
And though it's true to say,
I killed her husband – father too –
I'll have her anyway.

'And not because I love her –
But she could aid my plan;
But hold, I run before my horse,
A too impatient man...

'For Clarence is yet much alive
And still King Edward reigns –
Only when they're dead and gone
Can I then count my gains.'

~ ~ ~

Now with Clarence in the Tower
One hurdle was removed;
In Richard's path towards the crown,
His chances were improved.

As long as he could find a way
To convince the king
That Clarence was a guilty man,
Well then, from this he'd wring...

An order for poor Clarence
To be condemned to death.
'For I will have my way in this,'
He vowed beneath his breath.

But now he's set to win a wife,
But what a devilish plan!
For as we know he wished to wed
The lovely Lady Anne.

Richard had killed her husband;
And her husband's dad as well,
So she thought Richard Gloucester
Had earned his place in hell.

He'd carried out these murders
In the conflict known
As the Wars of the Roses –
A fight for England's throne...

'Twixt the House of Lancaster,
And the House of York;
A conflict in which neither side
Had been prepared to baulk.

Her husband's father once was king –
Henry the Sixth he'd been –
And so we enter now upon
A quite amazing scene.

Despite these two foul murders
Still Richard sought a way
To marry lovely Lady Anne
And he'd brook no delay.

For she was well connected,
Her hand would help him get
The throne of England for himself,
And so he cast his net.

He found her with a coffin,
Emotions deep and raw,
For it contained the last remains
Of her dear father-in-law.

And as she walked along she sobbed,
Her tears came in a flood;
'Cursed be the hand that made these holes
And spilt this precious blood.

'The murderer of King Henry
And of my husband too –
How he has made me shed such tears
By foully killing you.'

She cursed Richard of Gloucester,
She cursed his hated name;
She left no-one in any doubt
Of where she laid the blame.

Then from the shadows there appeared
A fiend in human form,
The sight of which made Lady Anne
Rage furiously and storm.

For it was Richard Gloucester
That she saw standing there.
She cried, 'How could you come here now,
How could you even dare?'

Richard addressed the bearers,
His face a solemn frown:
'You that bear the king,' he said,
'I bid you lay him down.'

'Oh, black magician!' Anne cried out.
'Don't stop our worthy deed,
Not when it was your filthy hand
That made King Henry bleed.'

'Set down your coffin,' Richard cried,
'And do not question why,
Or all you bearers here this morn
Will with King Henry lie.'

The coffin was set down in haste,
Then Anne began to yell.
Her words were filled with scornful hate,
She really gave him hell.

She cried, 'Foul devil, leave us here.
Leave us alone, I say,
For you can turn a happy world
Into a dismal day.

'You who had such dreadful power
O'er Henry's body here,
Cannot too own his very soul –
So leave us with his bier.

'And so I say begone gross wretch,
For you've brought on a flood –
Inhuman and unnatural –
Of gushing, flowing blood.

'You are the very devil;
A fiend in human guise;
For this is all your butchery
We see before our eyes.'

But Richard just deflected
Her every single word;
He took her accusations
As though they'd not occurred.

He simply paid her compliments,
And so her anger boiled;
The more he uttered honeyed words
The more that she recoiled.

He finally admitted,
'Your husband and the king,
I killed them both – and yes, I know
It was an evil thing...

'But my response, I did it –
Committed this high treason –
Merely out of love for you;
This was my only reason.'

She wailed, 'You killed my husband!'
He said, 'To make you free!
To find a better husband and
That better man is me!'

She spat upon him saying,
As spit flew in his face,
'I wish that it were poison.'
He said, 'From such a place...

'Poison would be, oh, so sweet.'
She sighed amid her cries,
'Get from my sight, you loathsome toad,
For you infect my eyes.'

She said she hated him so much,
Entirely and above
Anyone she'd ever known:
Still he professed his love.

Then Richard, laying bare his chest,
Exclaimed, 'Avenge your lord,
Likewise the monarch whom I killed.'
Then handed her his sword.

'Don't hesitate,' he cried. 'I killed
King Henry – yes it's true.
I also killed your husband,
Spurred by my love for you.'

'Though I wish your death,' she wailed,
'I cannot kill you here.'
'Then bid me kill myself,' he cried.
'I'll do it, have no fear.'

'No, no! Put up your sword,' she groaned.
He said, 'As I'm to live,
Take this ring, in fair exchange
For love you soon will give.

'For tell me I can have some hope.'
'All men can hope,' she said.
He replied, 'This I will do
Until I share your bed.'

She sighed, 'If only I could see
What lies within your heart;
I'll take this ring but don't you dare
Think by this I impart...

'That I'll give anything to you
For all the time I live,
Because it is well said – I think –
To take is not to give.'

So Lady Anne took up his ring
Then disappeared from sight.
When she had gone he praised himself –
As well indeed he might.

'Was ever woman won this way?
Was ever woman wooed?
Did ever man attempt to win
A woman in this mood?

'She has now forgiven me
In spite of my great wrong,
So I will have her now for sure –
But I'll not keep her long!

'And it is quite amazing
That I have turned her round
While she was on her way to place
King Henry in the ground.

'The bleeding witness to my hate
Is there for all to see,
And yet she still has turned her eyes
To look with care on me.

'She knows I killed her husband
And though her hate is strong,
And though she feels quite reasonably
I've carried out great wrong...

'And even though I'm ugly,
Why, still I've changed her mind;
It seems in time, to my bad deeds
The lady will be blind.

'Has she forgot already,
Prince Edward, her brave lord,
Who I but three short months ago
Stabbed fiercely with my sword?

'A sweeter, gentler, better man
Never did exist,
But now I think my evil charms
The lady can't resist,

'And so she cheapens her sweet self,
Excusing my gross crime
Of cropping that sweet prince's life
While he was in his prime.

'So if she turns her thoughts to me,
It maybe proves that I
Have been quite wrong about myself.'
He said this with a sigh.

'Perhaps I'm better looking than
I ever thought before,
So now I'll buy a mirror and
Cavort around the floor;

'I'll buy myself expensive clothes,
But till I buy a glass –
I'll pray for sun so I can see
My shadow as I pass.'

~ ~ ~

King Edward's wife, Elizabeth,
Upon a fraught filled day,
Was talking with Lord Rivers
And his friend Lord Grey.

Lord Rivers said, 'Be tranquil ma'am,
I'm sure his Majesty
Will soon recover normal health –
Yes, patience is the key.'

Then Lord Grey spoke to her too,
'You'll make things worse with worry;
There's really nothing to be gained
By getting in a flurry.'

The queen looked most concerned, downcast,
And with a groan she said,
'What would become of me, good lords
If our dear king were dead?'

Grey said, 'Why then my royal queen
You lose a husband so
That really is the end of it,
There's nothing more to know.'

But she replied most nervously,
Her voice held some alarm,
'The loss of my dear husband
Could cause a deal of harm.'

Grey looked to reassure her.
'You have a son,' he said,
'Who will be there to comfort you
When our great king is dead.'

The queen's face began to crumple
And then she looked away,
But she composed herself and then
She had these words to say.

'My son's still young and it's too soon
For him to rule this land,
And Richard Gloucester is the one
Who'll be the guiding hand.

'He will have the power and he
Loves neither me nor you,
And so it's anybody's guess
What that sly duke will do.

'I do not trust him – that is why
I worry and I fret.
I pray the king will soon be well –
That he won't die just yet.'

~ ~ ~

But what about poor Clarence?
What has become of him,
Imprisoned in the Tower on
A monarch's fickle whim?

He's going to get two callers
Who steal there in the night,
And sadly ill-used Clarence
Will get a dreadful fright.

They carry a death warrant
Initialled by the king.
It's all a travesty because
He hasn't done a thing.

But having signed the warrant for
The brother once held dear,
(And truly it was based upon
A quite unfounded fear)...

The king had changed his mind and so
He'd quickly sent another
To tell the keeper of the Tower
Not to kill his brother.

But it will come as no surprise
That Richard – foul and mean –
Had stopped the second message, found
A way to intervene.

And so the murderers approached
Duke Clarence in his cell;
They both were dressed in black and looked
Like evil ghouls from hell.

They quickly showed the jailor
The order from the king.
He read it very carefully,
Said, 'I won't ask a thing;

'I'd rather have no knowledge
Of what the king intends;
Here is the key, I'll leave you now,
He's in your care, my friends.'

He gave a murderer the key
And then he went away.
The evil pair then spoke and this
Is what they had to say.

One asked, 'So should we kill the duke
While he is fast asleep?'
The other said, 'When he awakes
He'll think our action cheap...

'For acting thus is cowardly.'
The first one said, 'Nay nay!
For he won't wake until he finds
That it is Judgement Day.'

And then he said, 'Are you afraid?'
The second, ''Tis a whim –
But I'm afraid I might be damned
For coldly killing him.

'The warrant makes it legal,
Yet conscience bothers me.'
The first one said, 'Just think upon
Our fat and handsome fee.'

'I forgot the fee,' the other said.
'Let's kill him right away!'
'So where's your conscience now?' his friend
Was very quick to say.

'Why in the Duke of Gloucester's purse,'
The second one replied.
'And if your conscience should return?'
The second one just sighed.

'Why then I will ignore it,
For conscience has the power
To make a coward of a man –
Cause him to baulk and cower.

'He cannot steal without concern
For it accuses him,
Or swear out boldly with no fear
For it has hold on him.

'He cannot take his neighbour's wife
For it will soon detect him,
He cannot act dishonestly
Without its weight on him.

'And so, enough of this my friend,
It is no time to shirk,
Put conscience in your pocket now
And let us go to work.'

They stole into the duke's grim cell;
Though neither of them spoke –
Clarence stirred and groaned and then
The poor, doomed duke awoke.

He saw the two fiends – knew at once
That he had much to fear.
He said, 'Your eyes do threaten me –
So why have you come here?'

The second murderer tried to speak,
He said, 'We've come to... to...'
'To murder me?' cried Clarence.
They said, 'Aye – murder you!'

Clarence said, 'You scarcely have
The hearts to tell me so –
And therefore you can't have the hearts
To strike a killing blow.

'And how have I offended you?
I haven't done a thing.'
They said, 'We have no quarrel
But you've upset the king.'

The duke replied, 'I love the king,
Why does he want me dead?
I've never been disloyal.
I care for him,' he said.

'Send for my brother Gloucester.
I beg you, sheathe your knife.
He will reward you handsomely
If you will spare my life.'

A murderer replied and thus,
'"Twas Richard sent us here.'
Clarence cried, 'It cannot be,
I know he holds me dear.

'Why, when I saw him recently
He held me by the arm
And promised me, and faithfully
He'd save me from all harm.

'He vowed that he'd do anything
And everything for me,
That he would go to Edward –
Get him to set me free.'

A murderer then said, 'And that
Is what he means to do,
To set you free in heaven,
This is his gift to you.

'But now my lord, make peace with God.'
He heaved a mournful sigh,
'For you must now prepare yourself –
It's time for you to die.'

One murderer then cried aloud,
'Look to your back, my lord.'
The other said, 'Take that!' And then
He stabbed him with his sword.

'To make quite sure he's dead,' he said,
'This stabbing I'll combine
With drowning in the butt within
That's filled with malmsey wine.'

The second murderer recoiled.
He cried, 'O bloody deed!
How savagely he's been dispatched,
How sad to see him bleed!

'I wish that I could wash my hands
Of this foul act I've seen.'
His partner said, 'Gloucester shall know
How tardy you have been.'

But he replied, 'Here take my fee –
Tell Gloucester what I say.
For I repent the duke is slain.
And now I shall away.

'For mayhem will descend when once
It's known that he is dead.
I only wished I'd taken steps
To save the duke,' he said.

~ ~ ~

King Edward was distraught when told
That Clarence had been killed.
He saw his first instruction had
Most sadly been fulfilled.

He had no way of knowing,
Richard had intervened.
The king declared he'd loved the duke
Since Clarence first was weaned.

He cried, 'The order was reversed,
So how is Clarence dead?'
'He died by your first order,'
Wily Richard slyly said.

'It must have gone by messenger
With wings upon his feet;
The second message though was borne
By someone not so fleet.'

King Edward spoke of Clarence –
Such grief was in his tone,
'When anger was upon me
Why did it stand alone?

'Why did nobody tell me?
Remind me of the fact –
That Clarence was a loyal friend,
Always there to act...

'On my behalf – a brother dear,
So loyal to the crown;
And no-one here spoke up for him,
You all have let him down.

'And I did not speak to myself
To plead for his sweet life,
And now I fear this act will bring
Destruction, woe and strife.'

The king then left and Richard had
The brazen gall to say,
'Clarence will be avenged by God,
Upon some future day.'

And then he said, 'Let's to the king,
And once we're there we'll see
If we can bring some comfort
With our fine company.'

~ ~ ~

And now we look upon a scene
As sad as any known,
As Clarence's two children grieve
At being left alone.

They are being counselled –
With sympathetic talk –
By their kindly grandmama,
The good Duchess of York.

And then the queen, King Edward's wife,
Her hair a tangled mess,
Comes rushing to the chamber
In evident distress.

'What's up?' the duchess asked the queen.
The queen just beat her head.
'Edward, my lord, your son, our king,
Has passed away,' she said.

'What will become of all of us?
How will the branches grow?
When now the tree that was the king
Is laid so very low.'

She cried great tears of sorrow, but
Earl Rivers, who was there,
Said, 'Get a hold upon yourself –
There's danger to beware.

'The king is dead and though we grieve
You *must* act right away:
Summon your son Prince Edward now –
Oh, bring him here, I pray.

'Let him be crowned immediately,
While in control and able;
Do it now with all good haste
To keep the kingdom stable.

'For in your son your safety dwells –
In young Prince Edward's throne;
In dead King Edward's grave there lies
Just sorrow – that alone.'

But then a brooding presence came
Into the mourning room;
Upon a scene of deep despair
He shed a further gloom.

For there stood Richard Gloucester,
A dark and huddled form,
Crouching whilst suppressing
An inward raging storm.

He approached the queen and said,
'We all of us have cause
To mourn our dear, lost shining star…
But, madam, prithee pause.

'All the crying in the world
Can give but small relief;
However much you wail and moan
It will not ease your grief.'

He slowly moved around the room
Exuding sympathy.
He said, 'My brother's sudden loss
Is such a blow to me'

It was of course an empty show;
He played the fawning lamb.
His motives were quite insincere,
An ostentatious sham.

They all agreed the youthful prince –
Without undue delay –
Should be brought back to London;
Indeed, come right away.

The matter settled, they all left,
But Richard stayed alone –
Save for the Duke of Buckingham,
The only friend he's known.

Buckingham told Richard,
'Now to avoid the worst –
We must make sure we reach the prince
And his young brother first.'

Richard whispered quietly,
'It's time to throw the dice
To win the throne of England, so
I'll act on your advice.'

~ ~ ~

Prince Edward came to London,
He joined his brother there,
And now they very soon became
A somewhat anxious pair.

Their uncle, Richard Gloucester
Met them there as well,
And they were eager now to hear
All that he'd have to tell.

Prince Edward asked his uncle,
'Where is the queen, my mother?
And what do you intend to do
With me and my dear brother?'

'You will be cared for,' Richard said,
'You'll stay within the Tower,
And there you will be housed until
Your coronation hour.'

Prince Edward looked most troubled,
A frown upon his face.
'I do not like the Tower,' he said.
'I really hate the place.'

Then his brother, Duke of York,
Spoke up and said, 'Oh dear!
The Tower is such an awful place –
There's so much there to fear.

'For I've been told, in dead of night
The corridors play host
To angry fiends they say include
Our Uncle Clarence's ghost.'

Prince Edward then said bravely,
'I fear no uncle dead.'
'Nor one that lives, I trust, young sir,'
His Uncle Richard said.

The prince replied, 'I hope not too,
But let us now depart
Unto the Tower, to where I go
With very heavy heart.'

~ ~ ~

And now a meeting's taking place;
Several lords are there
To plan the coronation –
But one there should beware.

Says Hastings, 'Well, my noble lords
We are all rightly bound
To set a day when Edward,
Our young prince, can be crowned.'

Ely's bishop then spoke up,
He said, 'I'd have to say
That tomorrow surely would
Be just the ideal day.

'What would the Duke of Gloucester think?
Now Buckingham – you know
His mind as well as anyone.'
Buckingham said, 'Oh?

'Although we know each other well,
I do not know his mind,
But Hastings you and he are close –
Perhaps you'd be so kind...

'To give us guidance here today.
Whatever should we do?'
Lord Hastings smiled and warmly said,
'My lord – my thanks to you.

'I know that Gloucester holds me dear,
And though we've not had chance
To set a coronation date,
I think if you advance...

'A date you think is suitable –
Well, I'll agree the same,
And do it on the duke's behalf –
I'll do it in his name.'

Then Ely spoke, 'Here comes the duke,
Arriving right on cue.'
Richard smiled at everyone
As he came into view.

Buckingham said, 'It's fortunate,
A very lucky thing,
That you've arrived, for we discussed
The crowning of the king.

'My Lord Hastings spoke for you.'
'Oh did he?' Richard said.
'Well no man can be bolder or
Know just what's in my head.

'But Buckingham – a word with you.'
He took him from the room,
And there in private spoke to him,
His face enmeshed in gloom.

'Hastings has been sounded out
About my plan,' he said.
'And he has vowed he'll not agree;
He'd rather end up dead.

'He'd rather lose his head than see
Young Edward lose the throne.
I think his loyalty's misplaced,
For Hastings has now shown...

'That he will ne'er support our cause,
And thus his wish,' he said,
'Shall be fulfilled – I'll see it done,
For I will have his head.'

And so they then returned and now
Richard changed his mood,
And on a trumped up, silly charge,
Contrived, unfair and crude...

He called Lord Hastings 'Traitor!
For he's done me great wrong;
He's schemed against my person
And done it all along.

'And now by good Saint Paul, I swear
I'll not eat lunch today
Until I see his head removed –
So do it right away.'

'Woe for England,' Hastings cried.
'I have been too remiss,
I should have seen this coming and
Then put an end to this.'

Then Ratcliffe spoke. He said, 'Enough!
You traitorous, sly sinner,
Make a short confession for
The duke now wants his dinner.'

'Miserable England,' Hastings cried.
'I prophesy great crime
Against you all from Richard;
A truly wretched time.

'But so be it, now take me hence;
Lead me to the block,
Then bring my head so Richard can
Before he eats – take stock.

'But I predict that those who smile
At my poor severed head,
Will follow me in briefest time –
They too will soon be dead.'

~ ~ ~

Once the princes were within
The Tower, shut away,
Richard spoke to Buckingham;
He had these words to say.

'We must arouse the populace,
We must do everything
To make them feel quite happy
About my being king.

'So go, address the rabble,
And to them all proclaim
The princes aren't of royal blood;
They have no rightful claim.

'You must declare them bastards – say
Their father, the late king,
Was no true monarch – that he lied
About just everything.

'And spread the rumour to the crowd
That when my devious mother
Fell pregnant with the now dead king,
With Edward – my late brother,

'Well, at the time that this took place,
Tell them, that by sheer chance –
My dear father was away
Attending wars in France.

'And so with not much effort
The folk will come to see
Edward's illegitimate –
But do this carefully;

'Touch this very softly and
Be vague in what you say,
Because my mother's still alive;
Be gentle, please, I pray.'

Buckingham replied, 'My lord,
Fear not, for I shall be
An orator of eloquence,
And I will make the plea…

'As if I spoke there for myself.'
And to the duke he bowed.
Richard said, 'If all goes well,
Then bring the fickle crowd…

'For audience to where I'll be,
With learned bishops, so
The people gathered will perceive
My piety on show.'

Buckingham left and Richard spoke
Words for himself alone.
'I must take further action now
But do this on my own.

'I'll write a secret order
That has a savage bite;
To keep dead Clarence's two brats
Safely out of sight.

'Also to forbid that none
Have the chance to see
My brother Edward's princely sons
Without recourse to me.'

And so with care and step by step
He planned by devious ways,
To claim the throne of England – and
To have it within days.

~ ~ ~

So Buckingham addressed the crowd
Who gathered there to hear,
But they all stood in silence,
And no-one raised a cheer.

He spoke about the princes,
Tried deftly to defame
Their honoured reputation
And blacken their good name.

He said, 'They're illegitimate,
They cannot claim the crown.'
He did most everything he could
To put the princes down.

He cried, 'Richard of Gloucester!
Now he's the man to reign.'
The crowd just stood in silence, so
He yelled it out again.

He cried, 'God save King Richard!
No-one else will do.'
But getting such a poor response
He silently withdrew.

~ ~ ~

Richard was beside himself
On hearing how the crowd
Had sullenly rejected him;
He cursed them all out loud.

Buckingham then calmed him down,
He quelled his great tirade.
He said, 'My lord, it's time to act
Like a reluctant maid.'

He outlined then his devious plan,
Which made sly Richard smile.
The scheme appealed for it was honed
With cunning, care and guile.

Buckingham went before the crowd,
Then summoned Richard there.
But a message came straight back –
He was at fervent prayer.

'Richard's not King Edward,'
The pious message said.
'He doesn't waste his precious time
In a lascivious bed.

'He kneels in meditation,
His soul of one accord
With holy hermits everywhere –
He's praying to the Lord.'

Another message then was sent,
Again the answer came –
And, no surprise, its contents were
In every way the same.

And so he tried a final time;
He sent another word.
What happened at this third attempt
Was really quite absurd.

Upon a balcony above
Came Richard, book in hand,
A bishop either side of him
Who each looked rather grand.

Buckingham called out aloud,
He begged him to come down
And greet the people waiting there
And to accept the crown.

Richard listened to his pleas
But kept on saying, 'No.
I am not worthy to be king,
And this you surely know.'

But gradually he came around.
He said, 'Since you all ask,
I will accept reluctantly
This very daunting task.

'It is a heavy burden
You buckle to my back,
But I will suffer this great load
And never ever slack.'

And so with protestations
This two-faced, cunning thing
Allowed the crowd assembled there
To choose him for their king.

Cried Buckingham, 'Long live the king,
The crown we'll now bestow.'
Dissembling, Richard answered,
'It seems you'll have it so.'

And to the bishops he then said,
'Before I start my reign
Let us return in haste unto
Our holy prayers again.'

~ ~ ~

And so they crowned him England's king;
Anne, now his wife, made queen,
In splendid pageant quite as fine
As any ever seen.

So everything he had desired
Had finally occurred,
For now he sat upon the throne,
King Richard, England's third.

Once king he spoke to Buckingham
And said, 'I wish to thrive,
But this is very difficult
While Edward is alive.'

Buckingham did not perceive
The plan in Richard's head.
'Let me be plain,' the king cried out.
'I want the princes dead.'

Richard saw that Buckingham
Did not approve the thought
Of yet another bloody deed
At this, the royal court.

So in that moment Richard turned
On Buckingham, his friend.
He thought, 'His days advising me
Are coming to an end.'

But Richard was determined
The princes now should die.
He summoned Sir James Tyrrel
And asked him with a sigh…

'Do you dare kill a friend of mine?'
Said Tyrrel, 'This I'd do,
And yet in truth I'd rather kill
Two enemies for you.'

Richard said, 'These enemies
Disturb each waking hour;
Tyrrel, I mean those princes who
Are locked up in the Tower.'

'Give me the means to reach them,'
Tyrrel answered, 'And for sure,
I will dispatch them right away:
They'll trouble you no more.'

Richard said, 'Now with this pass
You'll get into their cell,
So I rely on you to do
This act and do it well.

'And once the deed is truly done
And clear for me to see,
I will reward you handsomely
And draw you close to me.'

~ ~ ~

And so within an hour or two,
When dim had grown the light,
Tyrrel sent two men to kill
The boys that very night.

They crept into the princes' cell
Like wolves who stalk a hare,
And then with murderous villainy
They smothered them both there.

Once the deed was carried out –
Killed foully as they slept –
The evil, bloody murderers
Were so upset, they wept.

One said, 'They lay like gentle babes,
A prayer book at their side;
It is no wonder that we both
Have broken down and cried.'

But cry or not, the deed was done.
Came Tyrrel to the king.
And Richard, when he saw him asked,
'Is it good news you bring?'

Tyrrel answered, 'Yes, my lord.'
The king asked, 'Are they dead?'
'I saw their lifeless bodies sire
And buried too,' he said.

~ ~ ~

King Richard, with these murders done,
Was not quite finished yet.
He now desired to change his wife –
And his resolve was set.

He did away with poor Queen Anne
And Buckingham had fled.
The king no longer favoured him;
He feared now for his head.

For Buckingham had asked the king
To give him a reward:
'For helping you to gain the throne,
For risking all, my lord.'

But Richard was ungrateful –
He had these words to say:
'I'm not in giving mood right now,
Don't feel that way today.'

Buckingham was sorely vexed
And did all to attempt
To get to know the reason
For Richard's cold contempt.

He wracked his brains and spoke out loud,
Did all to understand;
The actions of King Richard seemed
Just mean and underhand.

'Is this how he gives just reward
For all the many ways
I've tried to aid his selfish plans?
Is this how he repays?

'For did I help to make him king
To have my wish refused?
Did I do all the things I did
To be so badly used?

'Oh let me think of Hastings
And let me then be gone,
To Brecknock while my fearful head
Is still securely on.'

Thus Buckingham saw clearly
Things didn't look too good,
So he had fled into the night,
As quickly as he could.

~ ~ ~

And these events signalled the end
For dark Richard the Third,
As news began to spread abroad
Of all that had occurred.

And Buckingham now raised a force
To fight his former friend;
And many forces now conspired
To bring about his end.

For Henry, Earl of Richmond,
Had then by happy chance
Landed with his army –
He'd come across from France.

So both these mighty armies
Combined with just one aim:
To rid the world of Richard –
Their purpose was the same.

But a little while before
The battle would be fought,
Poor, unhappy Buckingham
Tragically got caught.

He was shown no mercy,
For Richard wished him dead,
So he was executed
By chopping off his head.

~ ~ ~

The Earl of Richmond made his way
To England's heartland then
He spoke unto his army –
To all his bold, brave men.

'We've marched across this tortured realm
But now I have heard news,
That Richard Gloucester is quite close –
It's time for him to choose...

'Engage with us and boldly fight,
Or just to turn and run,
But I believe our triumph here
Has truly just begun.

'And by this bloody trial of war
We will with luck release
This realm from in a tyrants grasp
And gain a lasting peace.

'So my men arouse your hearts
And let your spirits lift,
And in God's name, we'll march ahead
And make our victory swift.'

~ ~ ~

Meanwhile Richard's mind is set,
He'll stand and never yield,
And orders that his tents be pitched
Right there on Bosworth Field.

And then he speaks unto his lords,
'Bring the finest men you can –
Men of sound experience –
To make our battle plan.

'And let us not lack discipline,
Make haste, brook no delay,
For my brave lords, tomorrow –
We have a busy day.'

~ ~ ~

The night before the battle
Richard did his best
To gather his resources
And get a little rest.

But as he slept there fitfully
Some ghosts came unto him;
They came with messages that were
Doom laden, stark and grim.

The first was good Prince Edward's ghost,
King Henry's much loved son,
And he reminded Richard
Of the dire deed he'd done.

He said, 'You stabbed me in my prime –
At Tewkesbury – that's why
I come to you tonight to say,
Despair therefore, and die.'

Then King Henry's ghost appeared,
He said, 'Think every hour
Of how you stabbed me cruelly
When I was in the Tower.

'You punched my body full of holes,
And that Gloucester is why,
Henry the Sixth has come to say,
Despair foul fiend and die.'

Then Clarence's poor ghost arrived,
He said, 'My hoped for goal
Is that I will sit heavily
Tomorrow on your soul.

'I that was drowned in malmsey wine –
By guile brought to my death,
Think of me in battle as
You face your final breath.

'And as you meet your rightful end,
And sigh your final sigh,
Remember Clarence and these words,
Brother – despair and die.'

And then the princes' ghosts spoke out.
'Yes uncle – rightly cower;
Dream about your nephews who
Were smothered in the Tower.

'Let us lie within your heart
And pull you down like lead,
And let us weigh you down with shame
Until you're justly dead.

'Your nephews souls now bid you
A terrible goodbye,
And tell you with one tortured voice,
Uncle – despair and die.'

And then he saw Lord Hastings there
Who said, 'You violent man,
Wake up tomorrow full of guilt
As but the wicked can...

'And end your awful, bloody days
Within the battle fray,
And think about Lord Hastings then
Upon that final day;

'And dwell upon your treachery
To one who didn't lie,
And then bad king, I say to you,
Despair – and then just die.'

Richard's wronged wife Anne appeared.
She sighed, 'Your wretched wife
Now comes to fill your sleeping hours
With ghastly thoughts and strife.

'I never had a quiet hour
When with you I did lie,
So in battle think of me –
And then despair and die.'

Then finally Lord Buckingham
Came unto the king,
His voice, it sounded terrible,
With such a fearsome ring.

He said, 'I was the very first
To help when you were down;
The first to give advice and aid
For you to gain the crown.

'In battle on the morrow
Keep me in your sight,
But as you sleep, dream horribly
Of death and blood tonight.'

Then Richard woke up in a sweat.
He cried, 'Oh now it seems
All those I've murdered in the past
Have come to me in dreams.

'No-one loves me that I know;
It seems, if I should die,
No-one will pity me for sure
Or give a sorry sigh.

'But I'll be brave in battle
And go at it pell-mell,
And either be a noble king
Or make my way to hell.'

~ ~ ~

A mighty battle now commenced
Upon fair Bosworth Field;
Each side determined that they'd win –
And neither one would yield.

The battle raged remorselessly,
The scene a field of blood,
Yet they fought on ferociously,
Upon a sea of mud.

Then in the midst of battle
Richard lost his trusty steed;
This is the moment that we hear
The desperate monarch plead...

'A horse! A horse! My kingdom
For a horse!' he yelled.
He knew that standing there on foot
He could be quickly felled.

The Earl of Richmond saw him
And there began a fight;
A test of courage, strength and will,
A truly stirring sight.

Their swords both clashed together
In a frightful fray,
Until the moment Richard fell –
Richmond had won the day.

With Richard dead upon the ground
The Earl inclined his head.
'The day is ours,' he cried aloud.
'The wicked dog is dead.'

And then the good Earl Stanley took
The crown from where it lay;
He offered it to Richmond
And had these words to say.

'Courageous Richmond – noble sire,
There's many here who'll tell
That you deserved to win this day
Because you fought so well.

'So take the crown that's truly yours;
Wear it – enjoy it too,
And my lord, make much of it
For it belongs to you.'

They crowned him then, King Henry,
The Seventh he became,
The first of all the Tudors
Who earned England great fame.

He said, 'This realm of England
Has wept a stream of blood,
Brought on it by an evil king,
A grim torrential flood.

'But now we say it's over –
The tyrant is now slain;
Let fair and prosperous days begin,
Let peace reign here again.'

But Arthur pleaded to be spared

KING JOHN

When King Richard – the Lionheart –
Died on campaign in France,
His brother John was quick to say,
'I think this is my chance...

'To have a try at ruling –
It's always been my hope
To be the king, for I believe
I've got the skill to cope.

'Yes, I can rule the country,
For I'll soon get the knack
Of reigning, but I'll make quite sure
To always watch my back.'

He never spoke a truer word
For trouble was in store,
Since Philip, who was King of France
Was now hell-bent on war.

For he believed Prince Arthur,
A nephew of King John,
Was the one the English crown
Should be bestowed upon.

And who could say he wasn't right?
For Arthur was the son
Of King John's older brother,
So he should be the one...

To claim the throne of England –
But his hopes all came unstuck
When John had grabbed it for himself:
The prince was out of luck.

Arthur at this time was young,
And some would surely say,
He really wasn't fit to reign
For many a long day.

Yet Philip wanted him in charge,
Insisting he'd be glad
If Arthur was made England's king –
He really liked the lad.

But no surprise, that bad King John
Would not give up the throne
For some pubescent, pimply boy;
A child not fully grown.

An envoy from the French arrived:
'Philip's prepared to fight.'
King John responded, 'Hear me well –
Then get out of my sight.

'Tell Philip I'll fight war for war.'
His words came in a flood.
'And I will match him sword for sword,
And also blood for blood.'

The envoy thus addressed, replied,
'King John, you may be sure,
That Philip will not stand for this,
Your actions will mean war!

'For Arthur should be king by right,
He is the one to rule.'
King John replied, 'Tell Philip this –
Just stick to playing boule!

'Tell him to keep his nose right out
Of England's state affairs,
For if he interferes this way
He'll soon be saying prayers.

'For I'll give him a bloody nose,
One that I freely bet
He'll find extremely painful and
He will not soon forget.'

Queen Eleanor, King John's mama
Then had the final word;
She commented with solemn face
On all that had occurred.

She said, 'I blame that Constance,
Arthur's ambitious mum
For moaning to King Philip who
Has now become her chum.

'It's she who's got the French involved
And stirred events up thus.
She's the one who is to blame
For causing all this fuss.'

And so it was not long before
King Philip's men laid siege,
To Angiers, a town in France –
Which had as royal liege...

The King of England, now King John,
And every living soul
Within the town paid court to him;
It was in his control.

But Philip laid out his demands;
He said, 'Angiers, I vow –
You'll come within the sphere of France;
You must surrender now.'

He told them very clearly,
'You have to do one thing,
And that is to accept right now
That Arthur is your king.'

And then he said, 'Once this is done,
And he's king of this town,
Well then I'll take the steps to give
Young Arthur, King John's crown.'

The citizens of Angiers
Would not accept this fate,
And so they cowered in the town
Behind their wooden gate.

But then an army came along
Approaching from the west,
And it was led by bold King John
Beneath an English crest.

King Philip calmly tells King John,
'You must now step aside
And give your throne to Arthur here.'
'Get lost!' King John replied.

Philip addressed Angiers then
And said, 'You must now choose.'
But they knew well, what e'er they did
They only stood to lose.

And so both armies now surround
This town, so small and fair;
The passions of two countries
Combine and end up there.

Philip tells the citizens –
Emotions all aflame –
'Arthur should be England's king.'
John makes his counter-claim.

'I am your king and Angiers
Is mine; I counsel you
That your allegiance is to me.'
What could the poor town do?

For they were in a quandary.
Whoever should they choose?
They were concerned their choice might prove
To be the one to lose.

They said, 'We will surrender
To the claim that's true –
To the country's lawful king –
So we say, which of you...

'Is speaking to us truthfully?'
Of course they each cried, 'Me!'
So how could this be sorted out?
What would the answer be?

Well, no surprise, the armies fought –
Then both claimed that they'd won.
Neither side was strong enough
To wholly overrun...

The other in the field, and so,
As it was getting late,
They had to stop the fighting and
Agree to a stalemate.

So then it was suggested,
Once they had called a halt,
That all this senseless bloodshed
Had to be the fault...

Of Angiers poor citizens,
'It's down to them, the swine.
Now let's attack them as one force,
Let all our troops combine.'

When the townsfolk heard of this
They very quickly saw
They'd have to find a way to stop
The fighting and this war.

So they proposed a compromise.
'Let Blanche, King John's fair niece
Wed France's heir, the Dauphin,
And bring about a peace.'

And so it was agreed forthwith;
The pact was quickly made.
But there were many mortified
By this expedient trade.

For Arthur's mother, Constance, felt
That she had been betrayed.
She thought the French king was a fool –
A bad deal had been made.

Though in the deal, King Philip gained
Control of much French soil –
Giving up her Arthur's claim
Made Constance's blood boil.

For in return King Philip vowed
He'd never now again
Push Arthur's right to England's crown:
In peace – King John could reign.

~ ~ ~

But then a cardinal from Rome
Arrived at court one day.
Pandulph was this fellow's name –
He had stern words to say.

Directing all his ire at John,
He spun things on their head;
With irritation in his tone
He turned to John and said,

'I do not like the man you've picked
To be the church's voice;
Canterbury's bishop there –
I do not like your choice.

'You should have asked me what I thought,
You really should have waited.
Change your mind or I will have
You excommunicated.'

John wouldn't take this lying down.
He had a fit of pique,
And said, 'Who does he think he is?
What an infernal cheek!'

And so he told the cardinal,
'You haven't got a hope
Of getting me to do your wish.
So tell that to the Pope.'

At this the cardinal cried out,
'This is no papal whim.
I shall not tolerate this talk.'
And he walked out on him.

He excommunicated John;
He kicked him from the church.
Then gleefully he smiled and said,
'That's knocked him off his perch.'

But John was not at all perturbed.
He just arranged a feast
And told his friends, 'I'll not be bossed
By an Italian priest.'

Then Pandulph made his way to France
And said to Philip there,
'If you don't break your pact with John,
Then also be aware...

'I'll excommunicate you too
If you don't heed my plea.'
So Philip broke his truce with John
To please the Papacy.

It's true that he was influenced
By the young Dauphin there,
Who told his father ruefully,
'I think you should beware.

'I feel you must give careful thought
To what would now be worse –
To lose proud England for a friend
Or suffer Rome's dread curse.'

~ ~ ~

So once again there is a war.
France and England fight,
To find out who will rule the roost –
Which king is in the right.

Young Arthur's fighting with the French
But, much to his dismay
He's caught and John declares that he's
'A serpent in my way.'

He orders that the boy should die,
Hubert de Burgh is told
To take firm steps to make quite sure
The boy does not grow old;

In other words, to take his life –
And this is not a bluff.
King John just wants poor Arthur dead;
He's really had enough.

But though the king has made it plain,
'De Burgh, kill him today.'
Good Hubert just informed the king,
'I'll keep him out the way.'

So for the moment Arthur lived
And though extremely scared,
He knew that for a while at least
His threatened life was spared.

But later back in England –
Where Arthur was in jail –
Hubert's ordered to perform
A deed that makes him quail.

He's told to take young Arthur's life.
Oh, such a ghastly thing –
To murder him – the order comes
From John, sad England's king.

But Arthur pleaded to be spared
And Hubert changed his mind.
From being set to kill the lad
He turned to being kind.

For he was truly overcome
By this good, saintly boy
Whose life so far had not been blessed
With any real joy.

He said, 'You'll have to hide young man –
King John, he wants you dead.'
The poor boy thanked him but was still
Borne down with awful dread.

Then Hubert went to bad King John
And, telling lies, he swore
That he'd fulfilled the king's dear wish –
That Arthur lived no more.

King John was happy with this news
But lords attending there
Now asked, 'How could you kill the lad?
How could you even dare?

'For royal blood runs through his veins;
He is your kith and kin.'
They told him he was guilty of
Committing mortal sin.

Unrest fermented in the land:
The people were on fire,
For hearing of poor Arthur's death
Filled them with rage and ire.

John called kind Hubert to him
And told him angrily,
'All this unrest is *your* fault,
It isn't down to me.

'For you're the one who killed the boy,
A young lad in his prime,
You're the cruel, dark murderer
Who carried out this crime.'

What a nerve to lay the blame
Upon poor Hubert so!
The king had been the one to say,
'Hubert, you must go...

'And kill young Arthur right away,
I want that young boy dead.'
'Do not despair – he's still alive,'
Then Hubert boldly said.

But now bad news arrives that tells
How Arthur tried to flee,
But jumping from the castle wall
He failed to grab a tree...

And from that dizzy height he fell;
The prince died there and then,
Leaving John the most despised
And hated of all men.

For everybody blamed the king.
They said, 'King John has spilled
Prince Arthur's noble, precious blood.
It's he who's had him killed.'

An army now invades from France,
And many English lords
Join with the French against the king;
They pledge their English swords...

To rid fair England of this man,
To throw him from the throne.
And now King John feels quite let down,
Abandoned – all alone.

So as the armies both prepare
To battle once again,
King John is feeling sick inside –
He's lost the will to reign.

He goes to Swinstead Abbey
And, once ensconced in there,
He is resolved to take a rest –
Might even say a prayer.

But while he's there a monk decides
The king is just no good.
He walks around the Abbey grounds –
Face hidden in a hood...

And quietly makes up his mind,
Though with a heavy sigh,
It would be best for everyone
If England's king should die.

And so he poisoned bad King John,
But as he passed away –
The English lords desert the French,
Come back on side that day.

And then another peace is made
As French troops all withdraw,
And once again we see the end
Of yet another war.

King John's son, Prince Henry,
Who's quite a decent lad,
Says, 'Leave me now in peace awhile.
I want to bury dad.'

And as we see King John's demise
There's just one other thing,
And that's to say, Prince Henry there
Became the English king.

And it was said at Henry's court,
'No-one, despite all ill,
Can ever conquer England's realm,
And no-one ever will.

'For England has no cause to fear –
Nor ever cause to rue –
If England has a decent king
And to that king is true.'

*Prince Edward then triumphantly
Displays the French king's crown*

EDWARD THE THIRD

Our tale begins as Edward, King
Of England makes the claim
That he should rule all France as well –
The French throne is his aim.

But it will come as no surprise
That John, who's France's king,
Declared, 'I've never ever heard
Of such a saucy thing.'

He sent the good Duke of Lorraine
To Edward there to say,
'You have no right to France and so
Just take your claim away.

'Instead, however you can be
In France a senior duke.'
King Edward up and answered him
With swift and stern rebuke.

'I soon shall come to France and take
Your kingdom – make it mine,
And then forever more it will
Be passed on down my line.'

But then King Edward's mind was turned
Onto another thing –
Which makes it very clear indeed
It's hard to be a king.

For David, King of Scotland,
Has flexed his royal might
And sent a force to England –
And they're prepared to fight.

As Edward there was thinking
Of France and what to do,
King David was besieging
A countess Edward knew.

She was at Roxburgh castle
And things looked bad indeed.
She was desperate for help –
She had a pressing need.

King Edward said, 'The Countess
Of Salisbury is my friend,
I will not contemplate that she
Should meet a rotten end.

'So I will go to Roxburgh
And punish all those Scots;
I'll finish off King David
And all his silly plots.'

Then turning to his much-loved son,
Prince Edward, who was known
As the Black Prince, he said to him,
'I trust to you alone...

'The task to raise an army
And then I think, perchance,
Across the English Channel you
Should go, and conquer France.'

With this all settled, Edward then
Set off that very day
For Roxburgh, where he soon found out
The Scots had run away.

The countess said, 'My precious liege,
Thank goodness that you're here.'
The king replied, 'You're quite safe now.
There's nothing more to fear.'

He really should have chased the Scots
But he was in a whirl
When he beheld the countess there –
She was a lovely girl.

And though he was a married man
He vowed that he would do
A thing quite out of order:
He'd do his best to woo...

The lovely countess whom he'd saved;
She'd surely prove to be
So pleased to gain attention
From such a one as he.

He walked around enraptured,
He sighed and spoke of love,
He said the apple of his eye
Was really way above...

All creatures in this mortal world –
That nothing could compare;
And if his love was not returned
He'd wither in despair.

He told his servant, Lodwick,
'I'm not prepared to quit,
And so I want you now to write,
Inspired by your wit...

'A poem that will stir the soul –
Such beauty fills my heart.'
'Is it a woman?' Lodwick asked,
As he prepared to start.

Edward cried, 'You fool! You knave!
It's for a lass, of course.
Oh, wretched man, did you believe
I bid thee praise a horse?'

Lodwick tried his best to write
A poem for the lass,
But in truth his every word
Was feeble, weak and crass.

So Edward grabbed the pen and wrote
Of love and pain and how
He loved the countess best of all,
That he must have her now!

But then the countess sashayed in,
She waltzed into the room,
And seeing Edward's mournful face,
Said, 'Why, my lord, such gloom?

'You look fed up and so morose,
Pray tell me, Highness dear,
If there is something I can do
To make that deep frown clear.'

Sneaky Edward saw his chance.
He thought, "I'll tell her how
To cheer me up, but first of all
I'll make her take a vow."

'Now will you promise me you'll cure
This sad unhappy man?'
The countess said, 'Of course, my liege,
I'll do the best I can.'

'Then be my mistress,' Edward cried.
'To love you is my goal.'
She cried, 'If I submit to you
I'll sacrifice my soul.

'I owe my husband faithfulness
As you owe to your queen;
To take you as my lover
Would be most base and mean.'

The king replied, 'You promised me
You would do all you could
To make me happy, so I thought
You clearly understood...

'That it was all agreed and set –
You'd honour this your vow;
So I demand that you fulfil
Your solemn promise now.'

But still the countess wouldn't budge,
So Edward, in a lather
Approached the Earl of Warwick,
Who was the lady's father.

He said, 'Instruct your daughter
To be my mistress now.'
The Earl reluctantly agreed
And with a sweeping bow...

He left the room and made his way
To his poor daughter fair;
He said, 'You can't refuse the king –
You'd be a fool to dare.

'It's best to lose your honour,
Not sacrifice your life.'
She cried, 'I have a husband and
King Edward has a wife.

'If I'm his mistress I betray
My loving husband's trust,
So I refuse to be a toy
For Edward's graceless lust.'

The Earl of Warwick was relieved —
His girl had proved to be
A fine, upstanding, moral wife.
He said, 'I'm pleased to see

'That you are so determined
To tell the king to go
And seek a mistress somewhere else —
That you don't want to know.'

And so, returning to the king
They both walked through the door.
He looked up hopefully and said,
'So tell me, what's the score?'

The countess said, 'I'll give to you
All that which you desire.'
The king looked then with lustful gaze —
His passions were on fire.

'But first we must remove those things
That stand there in the way
Of this our love – for my dear lord,
There is a price to pay.'

The king gazed at her quizzically –
What schemes were in her head?
'So what must we remove, my dear?'
He very softly said.

Without a word the countess then
Produced two long, sharp knives
And said, 'Between our love the thing
That stands is our own lives.

'Our deaths must come before our love.'
She offered him a knife.
Edward recoiled but she declared,
'I'll surely take my life...

'Unless you promise here and now
To never try again,
To have me for your mistress, sire,
For it is quite insane.'

At this the king perceived that his
Behaviour had been bad;
He saw he'd been a lustful fool,
A bounder and a cad.

He promised from that moment
He'd show his lust the door,
And treat her as an English rose
Henceforth – and evermore.

~ ~ ~

Then Edward made his way to France
To join the Black Prince there,
And met with France's reigning king
And to him did declare...

'I've come to France to stake my claim,
And ere the sun goes down,
I urge you step aside and give
This rightful king the crown.'

King John exclaimed, 'Pernicious wretch!
You foreigner! You swine!
I am the rightful king of France.
This kingdom is all mine.'

With all negotiations thus
Completely broken down,
Two armies there at Crecy field
Would battle for the crown.

And to the death they both would fight
To ascertain who'd own
The fair and favoured realm of France,
Who'd win the royal throne.

Before the battle, Edward called
His brave son to his side;
He gazed at him admiringly
And with a father's pride.

He said, 'As you prepare to go
To fight on Crecy field,
It is my solemn duty
To give you your first shield.

'A suit of shining armour,
A helmet and a lance;
Also a father's blessing, son –
Now win for me fair France.'

Prince Edward rode to battle,
Completely free of fears;
His father's final, loving words
Were ringing in his ears.

'You must earn your knighthood;
True honour must be won
In bloody, fearless fighting –
It is the way, my son.'

And in the dreadful battle
His father's words rang true –
Prince Edward there was fighting,
And how his courage grew.

But word is brought unto the king:
'We fear for your son's life.
He's in the thick of battle,
Deep in the fray and strife.

'Shall we rescue him, my lord,
Before it is too late?'
'No don't.' responded Edward,
'We'll all stay here and wait.

'For I have other sons, you know,
To comfort my old age,
And he must earn his spurs today
Upon this bloody stage.

'This is his chance to season
His courage and his might.
He'll either die today or earn
The right to be a knight.'

Harsh words indeed, but then the king
Knew 'twas the only way
His son and heir could thus become
An honoured man that day.

And so it was that later on
Prince Edward came and said,
'A victory we here have won ,
For all the French have fled.'

And then the king had more good news,
For he received the word
That yet another victory
Had recently occurred.

King David had been captured,
The Scots were on the run,
And so King Edward's forces
On two bold fronts had won.

But still he must remain in France –
The French weren't finished yet;
They still could field sufficient force
To be a serious threat.

The Black Prince now, once more prepares
To face the French again.
He's told they've gathered a huge force
On Poitier's great plain.

Lord Audley says, 'My royal prince,
We face a mighty test.'
But Edward laughs and clearly shows
That he's quite unimpressed.

And then a messenger arrives,
And to the prince does tender
A missive from King John that says,
'Be sensible – surrender!'

Again the Black Prince laughs and says,
'What an infernal cheek.
You tell King John, I do intend
To give his nose a tweak.'

Another message then arrives,
It comes from King John's son;
It offers Edward a fast horse
On which the prince can run.

And then a little gift arrives,
It's brought to Edward there;
A present from the French – it is
A holy book of prayer.

The inference is very clear;
'Black Prince – get on your knees,
And pray the good Lord up above
Gives notice to your pleas.'

Prince Edward merely scoffs and says,
'Remove this from my sight.'
And then he pulls his visor down
And so prepares to fight.

The battle starts and at one point
King Edward's told for sure,
The Black Prince has been wounded
And that he fights no more.

He says, and others tremble as
They hear their monarch speak,
'If he is killed, such vengeance I
Will very surely wreak.

'For the prince's funeral knell,
If it's confirmed he's dead,
Will be the piteous cries and moans
Of dying men,' he said.

But as he speaks a trumpet sounds;
Prince Edward then strides in.
He's bloodied and bedraggled but
He wears a buoyant grin.

King John is now his prisoner –
He stands there looking down;
Prince Edward then triumphantly
Displays the French king's crown.

He hands it to his father;
Then, standing proud and tall,
He shouts aloud to everyone,
'I tell you, one and all…

'I'll fight those French men any time,
And Spain and Turkey too;
And anyone who wants a fight,
Well, they can join the queue.'

Elated now with victory,
Success set him on fire.
He cried, 'I'll fight all those who dare
Provoke fair England's ire.'

King Edward calmly shook his head.
'Patience, my son,' he sighed.
'It's time to rest, for I believe
Too many men have died.

'And so I say, don't fret and fuss,
Don't fume and froth and foam.
It's time we sailed for England.
It's time that we went home.'

*In quite the finest set of clothes
The court had ever seen*

HENRY THE EIGHTH

Our story opens at the court
Of Henry – England's king,
And there we find three lords who speak
Of a momentous thing.

Their royal master, Henry,
The eighth that England's had,
Has just come back from France, where he –
The vain man – had been clad...

In quite the finest set of clothes
The court had ever seen;
The meeting was most dazzling,
The showiest there'd been.

For there the young King Henry
And France's young king too,
Competed with each other;
They each tried to outdo...

The other with their finery,
The splendour of their court,
And in amongst the glitter
There was much fun and sport.

This meeting has grown famous;
You may have heard it told
How these two men met at the field
Known as the Cloth of Gold.

For there was such great opulence
And splendour all on show;
Everything was bright and brash,
The whole field was aglow...

With shiny, sparkling armour,
Bedecking men so bold,
And pennants flying in the breeze
Of red and blue and gold.

And in amongst this dazzling sight
Two kings had walked abroad,
Dressed in their lavish finery,
They walked on that green sward.

Their garments had so glittered –
A sight there to behold;
That's why this pageant has been called
The Field of Cloth of Gold.

But as the lords there chat away,
Says Buckingham, 'Perchance,
This was too much extravagance
Just for a chat with France.

'It cost a lot of money,
We went right overboard.'
But Norfolk said, 'If I were you
I'd watch your tongue my lord.

'For Wolsey, Henry's cardinal –
He organised the thing,
And as you know, he's very close
And friendly with the king.'

Buckingham says that Wolsey
Is always on the make;
Though he pretends great piety,
He's really on the take.

'It's time the king was made aware
That Wolsey is a crook;
His two-faced lying attitude
Is something I'll not brook.'

He thinks, 'I'll tell King Henry of
The man's dishonesty,
And then, with luck, in gratitude
The king will honour me.'

~ ~ ~

Before the Duke of Buckingham
Can put his plan in place,
He is accused of treason,
Arrested in disgrace.

The cardinal's behind it –
And not without good reason;
He's set to get revenge and so
Accuses him of treason;

And though a trial is soon arranged,
It all becomes quite clear
That Henry wants him dead as well,
And will not deign to hear...

Lord Buckingham's defence, and so,
The duke is in a jam:
The court proceedings are absurd,
The trial is just a sham.

And so he was condemned and then
Beheading was his fate –
For gross disloyalty towards
The king and to the state.

As he was led away to face
Beheading on the block,
Poor Buckingham looked back on things
And gravely he took stock.

He spoke aloud most earnestly
And said, 'I'd have you know
That those who come to pity me,
Just hear these words then go.

'I have this day received the word,
A traitor, I must die;
But I declare in heaven's name
This judgement is a lie.

'And even as the axe comes down
Depriving me of breath,
I do swear that I do bear
No malice for my death.

'And to those few who loved me –
To those who showed me care –
I ask that as the axeman strikes,
You offer up a prayer.

'And with this one small sacrifice,
Whispered in words so soft,
You will assist the angels as
They bear my soul aloft.

'And now I say of Henry,
He made me a worthy man;
He bore me up to noble things
As only great king's can.

'But at a stroke, he cast me down
And put this friend on trial,
Accused of treason and though false,
He will brook no denial.

'Yet as I stand so close to death,
I see his regal face,
And beg that if you see the king,
Commend me to his grace.

'But now good people, I must leave
This world where pain runs rife,
For I must face the final hour
Of my long, weary life.

'And when, of something that is sad,
You would to others tell,
Then speak of how Lord Buckingham
Met his sad fate and fell.'

And then he said, 'Forgive me God.'
Then turned to everyone
And sadly breathed his last goodbye;
'Farewell, for now I'm done.'

~ ~ ~

Queen Katherine, the king's good wife
Thinks ill of Wolsey too.
She says, 'He's full of grasping greed,
Corrupt and false right through.'

And so against these goings-on
The king arrives to play;
A banquet and a splendid ball
Are taking place that day.

He enters and he walks around
And then, as if by chance,
He looks across at Anne Boleyn
With a romantic glance.

Lady-in-waiting to the queen,
She stands demurely there;
She shouldn't flirt with Henry,
She really should take care.

But then what can she do when he,
The king of everyone,
Winks and then commands that she
Should dance and have some fun.

~ ~ ~

So now the king has let his gaze
Fall lustfully upon
Young Anne Boleyn, and he's about
To pull, some say, a con.

For Henry now decides to say,
'The queen is not my wife.
I cannot carry on like this
And live a sinful life.

'My brother was her husband once —
I now see all along,
Though he is dead, for us to wed
Was absolutely wrong.'

But this, of course, was just a ruse,
A way to make the claim
His marriage was a living lie;
Divorce was now his aim.

The Papal legate comes from Rome.
The king hopes he'll endorse
His claim that Katherine's not his wife,
And grant him a divorce.

He hopes he'll say that when he wed
His brother's wife before,
The Pope will undertake to state
He broke the church's law.

That he's not really married to
Queen Katherine – that he
Was wrong to take his brother's wife,
Though she was by then free.

So Henry argued furiously
And with tremendous force,
His marriage wasn't legal;
They therefore must divorce.

And thus a public trial is called –
Queen Katherine pleads her case.
There is great sadness and disdain
Upon the good queen's face.

She says she is the rightful wife
Of royal Henry there.
She says, 'The way he's treating me
Is totally unfair.

'For heaven witness, I've been true
Through all upsets and strife;
I've always been most dutiful,
A true and humble wife.

'So how have I offended?'
Her voice was strained and shrill.
'I've always been compliant
And faithful to his will.

'And so I say, my lord, to you,
Why do you cause this fuss?
Why do you drag me here to court
And make such fools of us?

'I've been your faithful, loving wife
Through ups and down and tears,
And lived in strict obedience
For nigh on twenty years.

'And when at first we spoke our vows,
Upon our wedding day,
Did not those present all declare
It lawful? Speak I pray.

'For my dear father, King of Spain,
And your good father too,
Both took wise counsel everywhere
On what was right to do.

'And all spoke out and did proclaim
It was within the law.
So tell me Henry, husband dear,
What is this trial for?'

And then in desperation
She said, 'My only hope
Is to appeal to Rome itself;
To beg help from the Pope.'

A silence fell upon the court,
An all-pervading gloom,
And then Queen Katherine rose and stormed
In anger from the room.

The Papal legate sighed and said –
As he surveyed the scene –
'We cannot carry on without
The presence of the queen.'

And so that seemed the end of it.
King Henry sighed as well;
'She never was my legal wife...'
What lies that man could tell!

~ ~ ~

Now Wolsey, that old crafty fox,
Had plans that were his own.
He wanted bold King Henry
To share the English throne...

With a lady who was sister
To France's noble king;
He thought that this would prove to be
An advantageous thing.

But now King Henry was in love
With Anne Boleyn and so
There really was no chance at all
That he would want to know.

When Wolsey saw this was the case,
He thought, 'I won't endorse
His marriage plans' – so asked the Pope
To turn down the divorce.

His devious note was found, alas,
And taken with all haste
Unto the king, who looked at it
With evident distaste.

He asks fraught Wolsey to declare
He's loyal and he's true.
Wolsey replies, 'Your highness knows
I've always toiled for you.'

The king replied, 'You lie to me,
For Wolsey – with great stealth,
You've lined your pockets o'er the years
And so amassed great wealth.

'I've seen a list of all you own,'
The king then archly mocked.
'And I must tell you cardinal,
Your monarch's deeply shocked.

'These papers fell into my hands,
They're here for you to see,
They clearly show that you have not
Been looking out for me.

'You've filled your own great coffers –
You can read it all in here.'
Wolsey thought, 'Is this the end
Of my acclaimed career?'

Then when he's shown the letter
He'd written to the Pope,
He sees that he is cornered;
He gives up any hope...

And says, 'I've touched the highest point
My shoes will ever fill.
I see that from this glorious point
The way's now all downhill.'

He never spoke a truer word –
The king gave him the sack.
He said, 'Get out of here, right now,
And don't you dare come back.'

That was the end of Wolsey:
He left with downcast head,
And shortly after this they heard
The sad old man was dead.

~ ~ ~

Henry now divorced the queen;
His wife he just denied;
With ruthlessness the Tudor king
Threw Katherine aside.

And then he married Anne Boleyn –
The king had got his way;
And he arranged for her to have
A coronation day.

And it was said that Anne Boleyn
Looked quite the comely queen,
As gracious, fair and beautiful
As any woman seen.

And when the people looked on her
'Twas said by everyone
It truly was a noble thing
Their monarch had now done.

And such a mighty cheer rose up
That shook the very clouds;
A noise just like a tempest makes
Within a ship's great shrouds.

Hats and coats and doublets all
Were thrown into the air.
It was a truly happy day,
A joyful, grand affair.

At last young Anne Boleyn approached,
Serene and with restraint,
Unto the alter where she prayed;
She looked just like a saint.

She gazed up to the heavens,
And then she prayed again,
And all the people were as one
In hoping she would reign...

For many long and fruitful years;
They hoped she'd always be
Beside their monarch, there to give
Support and company.

Then Canterbury's archbishop,
Who was presiding there,
Bestowed the royal emblems
As he pronounced a prayer.

Edward Confessor's crown came first;
The rod and bird of peace;
The holy oil anointed her –
And then an ermine fleece.

The choir sang *Te Deum*,
The music was the best.
It stirred the soul and roused the blood
Of every noble guest.

Then once she was declared the queen
By Canterbury's priest,
The wedding party all repaired
To York Place for a feast.

So Anne was queen – but Katherine now
Was sick and close to death.
She wrote to Henry desperately,
And said, 'With my last breath...

'I beg you treat our daughter –
Young Mary – with respect;
Maintain her in the proper way
A princess should expect.'

And then she wrote, 'Dear Henry,
I now bid you goodbye.
Be certain in the knowledge that
I bless you as I die.'

~ ~ ~

Queen Anne is now in labour.
And then – one early morn –
A little baby daughter
Most happily is born.

The court comes for the christening;
They give their thanks and pray
For Henry's royal baby and
For this momentous day,

For it brings joy to everyone –
Such gaiety is brought
To Henry and his subjects,
And everyone at court.

Archbishop Cranmer says to all:
'Be of good cheer I pray.
A thousand, thousand blessings
This child brings us today.

'She brings unto this land of ours
Redemption from above,
Great peace and plenty, truth and joy,
Great harmony and love.'

King Henry really beamed at that;
He couldn't get enough
Of all this gilded flattery
And highfalutin stuff.

He then stood up and cried aloud,
Emotions all afire,
'When I'm in heaven I declare
That all I shall desire...

'Will be to gaze upon this child.
My soul will be abuzz —
I'll be so full of eagerness
To see what this child does!'

Prophetic words, it must be said:
In time the girl became
A truly great and much loved queen,
For she went by the name...

Elizabeth of England;
The first the realm had known.
For many happy, prosperous years
She'd sit on England's throne.

But that was all in time to come.
Now, as King Henry sighed,
The future Queen Elizabeth
Lay in her crib and cried.

THE ROMANCES

A splendid ship was fighting hard
To flee a watery grave

THE TEMPEST

Free your mind of everything,
Let imagination fly;
Soar with me above the sea,
Let's fly across the sky...

To an island that is lapped
By gentle, turquoise water,
Where an old man, Prospero,
Lives with his only daughter.

The girl is called Miranda and
Her memory has no trace
Of other human features
Beyond her father's face.

For she was young when they arrived,
They live there all alone;
So life with her old father is
The only life she's known.

~ ~ ~

Prospero studied magic, and
Through this had come to know,
An ancient witch once lived close by –
But died some time ago.

This hag was known as Sycorax;
She'd thought it quite a wheeze,
To lock up kindly spirits in
The bodies of large trees.

When Prospero had learned of this,
On coming to the isle,
He'd used his magic to release
The spirits from their trial.

These gentle, kindly spirits
Overcome with great relief,
All grew to love wise Prospero,
As did Ariel – their chief.

Blessed with a charming nature,
He was humorous and light,
Full of boundless energy,
A lively little sprite.

Alas, he had but one grave fault
Which no-one there could budge;
He'd tease an ugly monster
'Gainst whom he held a grudge.

This sad, lost soul was Caliban –
Whatever had he done?
Well, the witch had been his mother,
And he her only son.

When Prospero discovered him
He thought he was an ape,
He had such funny movements and
A very funny shape.

But Prospero had rescued him
For he was cold and weak;
He'd shown him many kinds of things
And taught him how to speak.

Still Caliban was not inclined
To work hard or be good,
Although they gave him easy tasks
Like gathering their wood.

He could be very lazy
And didn't care to work,
But Ariel took the utmost care
To see he didn't shirk.

Now Ariel could not be seen –
Except by Prospero's eyes –
So he would pinch poor Caliban
And then ignore his cries.

He'd sometimes turn into an ape
Which Caliban could see,
For Ariel could turn into
What e'er he wished to be.

He might become a hedgehog
With spikes that puncture skin,
And bumping into Caliban
Would try to prick his shin.

So he'd torment the monster
And Caliban would rue
The days he didn't do the tasks
That he'd been told to do.

~ ~ ~

Now Prospero made the spirits
Subservient just to him;
For they would carry out requests –
Indulge his every whim.

And through them he could order
A strange and bold decree,
Which could control the fickle winds
And rule the raging sea.

Performing these amazing feats
Became for him the norm,
So it was nothing special when
One day he raised a storm.

And in this tempest, harsh and wild,
Caught in a mighty wave,
A splendid ship was fighting hard
To flee a watery grave.

He showed his daughter, who cried out,
'Oh pity their distress.'
There was no doubt that Prospero
Had conjured up a mess.

For he had made the tempest howl,
He'd caused this raging show,
He'd made the mighty, roaring waves
And caused the winds to blow.

'Dear father, save their souls!' she cried.
'Oh, let them all be saved.'
Miranda was in quite a state –
She shouted, cried and raved.

'Don't be afraid my daughter,
And do not be alarmed,
I have arranged the tempest so
Nobody will be harmed.'

Then Prospero continued,
'I know the storm looks wild,
But I have manufactured it
For you, my only child.

'You know not where you came from,
You know but what you see,
You know I am your father but
That's all you know of me.

'Now tell, do you remember
A time before this place?'
Then, thinking carefully, she said,
'I just recall a trace.'

'I'm not surprised,' he answered.
'For as I've often told
When we arrived here on this isle
You were but three years old.'

Miranda said, 'It's very faint
Yet now and then it seems
I have a recollection,
When sleeping – in my dreams.

'I think I am surrounded
By maids – I can't be sure.'
Prospero went on quietly,
'Can't you remember more?'

'No dear father,' she replied,
'That's really all I can.'
He said, 'Before we came here –
I was duke of all Milan.

'You were a princess and enjoyed
A life devoid of care,
And you were destined as my child
To one day be my heir.

'Now I had a younger brother
I'd have trusted with my life.
He lifted from my shoulders
All daily toil and strife.

'So I retired to study,
Avoiding all my cares,
For Antonio, your uncle
Looked after my affairs.

'But he was acting falsely,
As soon I was to find –
While I was busy working
To improve my mind.

'For as he held the power
He then began to think,
That he himself should be the duke –
It happened in a wink.

'He planned to take my dukedom –
He really stooped that low –
And with the King of Naples
Who was my deadly foe...

'He laid a devious plan to take
Just everything I had.
I know it's hard to credit but
He really was that bad.

'Upon one dark and dreadful night
The King of Naples came
With an army and a plan –
Just with the awful aim...

'To capture us and take us
Far from our fair Milan.
The pair of them behaved just like
Only foul plotters can.

'They took us both aboard a ship
And we went out to sea,
And once we were some miles from land,
Why then they set us free.

'With neither tackle nor a sail
They placed us in a boat,
And then they cast us off to drift
Just aimlessly afloat.

'By luck, a friend, Gonzalo,
A counsellor of mine,
A faithful man of honesty,
Dependable and fine...

'Had seen that food and water –
A welcome little horde –
And all my wizard's magic books
Were safely placed on board.

'We drifted willy-nilly
For many countless miles.
And I was kept from giving up
By all your happy smiles.

'Our food gave out just at the point
We landed safely here.
So there you have the history
Of our misfortunes, dear.'

'Now father,' kind Miranda said,
'Take trouble to explain,
Why have you caused this tempest?
Why all this wind and rain?'

'By this storm,' her father said,
'I'm able to make sure,
Those foes of whom I spoke will now
Be washed up on our shore.

'By curious coincidence
The fates have thus conspired
To bring about a happening
That I have long desired.

'My brother sails upon that ship,
The King of Naples too;
This wicked pair tried to destroy
Not only me, but you.'

Prospero on looking up
Saw Ariel standing there,
So lest Miranda think that he
Was speaking to thin air...

He touched her with his magic wand,
And then without a peep
Her head inclined upon her chest
And she fell fast asleep.

'Well now spirit,' Prospero said,
'These questions would I ask:
Have you done all I wished and how
Have you performed your task?'

Ariel told him of the storm,
The fear of those on board,
How all of them were fighting hard
As his great tempest roared.

'I caused such bolts of lightning
And mighty thunder claps,
Even the bravest there was in
A state of near collapse.

'The king's own son, Prince Ferdinand,
Jumped straight into the sea;
The king believes his son is lost
But he sits on our quay.

'He is praying,' Ariel said,
'His father will be found,
But deep inside he really thinks
His father has been drowned.

'No hair upon his head is hurt,
He's fine – all this I saw –
His princely robes are wet, it's true,
But cleaner than before!'

'Gentle Ariel,' Prospero said,
'Now he has had a rinse,
Bring him to see Miranda,
For she must meet this prince.

'And tell me what has happened
To the king and to my brother?'
'They're searching for Prince Ferdinand
While they console each other.

'Although they think they saw him drown
Beneath a mighty wave,
They cannot quite accept he may
Have found a watery grave.

'I've caused the crew to fall asleep
So they're all still alive,
And I've ensured the ship rode out
The storm and did survive.

'It's safe now in our harbour;
I trust this pleases you?'
'It does indeed,' said Prospero,
'But there's more work to do.'

'More work!' cried Ariel in alarm,
'You know you promised me,
If I gave loyal service, you
Would gladly set me free.'

Prospero said, 'Why, what is this?
Remember when we met,
I saved you from vile Sycorax –
How quickly you forget.

'She'd locked you in an old pine tree.
For twelve years there you cried,
And then while still imprisoned –
Well, Sycorax then died.

'You'd still be there today if I
Had thought to let things be,
But when I heard your awful groans,
Why then, I set you free.

'And if I hear your whining voice
Ever more complain,
Well, I will place you in a tree
And lock you up again.'

'Forgive me my dear master,
Pay no heed to my demands,
I'm not at all ungrateful;
What are your new commands?'

'Obey me,' Prospero replied.
'Do all these things for me;
You'll see I'll keep my promise then
And I *will* set you free.'

He told the spirit next to check
On how the young prince fared.
When Ariel went back to him
He looked both tense and scared.

'Oh brave young man,' the spirit thought,
'I'll soon move you along.'
And losing not a moment he
Began to sing a song.

Ferdinand sat bolt upright
On hearing this strange singing,
Then followed the sweet music
With both his ears a-ringing.

Ariel's voice was heavenly;
It sang both high and low,
And led the prince towards the girl
And to old Prospero.

~ ~ ~

Miranda looking up beheld
A sight that made her ponder.
Prospero said, 'Now tell me, child,
What takes your fancy yonder?'

She said, 'Is that a spirit?
It has such lovely features.
Oh father, it is surely
The most beautiful of creatures.'

'He's no spirit,' Prospero said,
'He's just like you and I –
He eats and sleeps and breathes like us,
And like us too will die.

'This youth was travelling aboard
The tempest stricken ship;
He has been saved but not before
He took a little dip.

'And though there really is no doubt
He's very much relieved,
He thinks his friends are lost and so
He's also much aggrieved.'

Miranda thought the handsome prince
A passion-stirring sight,
And as she looked her tender heart
Was filled with pure delight.

Ferdinand, when he looked up
And saw her lovely face,
Could not believe what he beheld
In this forsaken place.

He thought the isle enchanted.
'You're a goddess!' he then said.
'I'm but a maid,' she answered as
She turned the brightest red.

Prospero was very pleased,
She'd met her shining knight,
For it was clear that both of them
Had found true love on sight.

But Prospero still had to test
The prince's love was true;
He called him 'Spy' and threatening said,
'I'll teach you what to do.

'You'll follow me,' he fiercely vowed,
'I'll tie you neck and feet;
You'll drink the water from the sea,
And roots are all you'll eat.'

'Indeed, I won't,' cried Ferdinand.
He drew his sword and said,
'You try to force these things on me
And you might end up dead.'

But Prospero waved his wand and so
A magic spell was sown –
In half a second Ferdinand
Was frozen like a stone.

Miranda cried aloud, for thoughts
Of love were in her head.
'Why are you so ungentle?
Have pity sir,' she said.

'This is the only man I've seen
Except, of course, for you,
But I believe he really is
As steady as he's true.

'I will vouch for him,' she cried –
Her heart was in a whirl.
'Be silent,' said her father, 'or
I'll punish you, my girl.

'You think that he has qualities
Which others can't display?
You're being very headstrong
To speak in such a way.

'For you have never had the chance
To know another man;
This youth might be no better than
Our servant, Caliban.'

Prospero was a cunning soul,
A wise and keen observer;
He did these things to test her love,
Her constancy and fervour.

He wasn't disappointed –
She was in a state of bliss;
She said, 'I do not wish to know
A better man than this.'

~ ~ ~

Prospero held the captive prince
Within a dismal cave;
Poor Ferdinand began to feel
That he'd become a slave.

He thought this even more when told
That there was work to do;
A hard and menial job, he felt
Demeaned him through and through.

It was a heavy task and yet,
He did the best he could:
Prospero instructed him
To pile up loads of wood.

The wizard had decided
It would be very wise
If the prince was set a test
Before he won his prize.

He didn't want the prince to think
Miranda's love came cheap,
And that is why he set the task,
To pile logs in a heap.

For if her love was won too soon
She would be valued less,
And so the prince was made to work
And suffer some distress.

Thus Prospero, quite quickly
Would see the prince unfurl
His character and then reveal
If he deserved the girl.

When Prospero told his daughter
What Ferdinand was doing,
She said she would be happier
If he had been a-wooing.

The wizard then took leave of her
And vanished into air.
Miranda went straight to the prince,
And said, 'This isn't fair...

'Do not toil so hard,' she begged,
'Father's now at work.'
But he replied, 'I mustn't stop,
I really dare not shirk.'

'I'll help you then,' the girl replied.
'You rest here by this tree.'
But there was nothing that would make
Prince Ferdinand agree.

As they began to talk the work
Of stacking logs slowed down,
And when he asked what she was called
Miranda pulled a frown.

For Prospero had warned her,
'Don't tell the prince your name.'
But this was just another part
Of his devious game.

For Prospero heard her give it.
He stood there by her side:
The wizard was invisible,
So had no need to hide.

And when he heard his daughter
Disobey him – this one time,
He wasn't angry with her
For such a paltry crime.

And when he heard the prince declare
He loved her far above
All other women in the world,
He blessed him for his love.

So happy that the prince now yearned
For Miranda's touch,
Happy that young Ferdinand
Was in love so much.

She said, 'I know no others,
But know one thing is true:
I do not wish for anyone
In all the world but you.'

At this her father nodded
In a way as if to say:
'I see my girl could be the Queen
Of Naples one fine day.'

And then Miranda said, 'Good sir,
I will, if you are free,
Become your loving wife, if you
Would care to marry me.

'I've never known another man
But swear my love is true;
So I can say with certainty
I want no-one but you.'

The prince declared, 'Miranda dear.'
He sank down on one knee.
'Here is my hand and willingly
Your husband I will be.'

'And I your wife,' the girl replied,
'And so I pledge my heart,
And vow that nothing in this world
Will e'er drive us apart.'

~ ~ ~

Some time later, Prospero
Said to the lovelorn pair
That he had heard them speak because
He had been standing there.

He called them to him and then with
A smile and nodding head,
And with a gentle gesture and
A kindly voice he said,

'Miranda, do not be afraid
That I have overheard,
For I approve most readily
Of every single word.

'And Ferdinand, now leave the logs,
Enjoy a well-earned rest,
The tasks I set were but a trial –
You've nobly passed the test.

'Take my daughter as my gift,
It's what I truly sought,
And it is what your loving heart
Has just as truly bought.'

He said he now had things to do,
He'd leave them all alone,
And they, of course, were very pleased
To have time on their own.

~ ~ ~

Prospero summoned Ariel
And asked him one more thing:
'What of my selfish brother and
His feckless friend, the king?'

Ariel said he'd left them
Both overcome with fear,
Scared by the strange and wondrous things
He'd caused the pair to hear.

He'd conjured up a banquet which
Appeared before their eyes,
Then turned into a monster
By way of a disguise.

He caused the feast to vanish and
To their amazement said,
'It's you who left Milan's true duke
And his sweet girl for dead.'

They cried in fear and terror
And said, 'It wasn't me.'
He said, 'You left the pair of them
To perish out at sea.

'And this is now the reason
You're suffering this way.'
Then both of them repented
Their actions on that day.

And Ariel told his master
He could not help but feel,
That what they said was from the heart,
Sincere and very real.

'Bring them here then,' Prospero said,
'For I'm inclined to fashion
A neat solution to this mess
And show them some compassion.'

Ariel straightaway brought back
Antonio and the king,
They were both confused – could not
Comprehend a thing.

They were also much afeared,
Borne down with grief and woe,
And neither of them recognised
Milan's duke – Prospero.

Gonzalo was there with them too –
You will recall I wrote
How he had helped wronged Prospero
By kitting out the boat.

So Prospero revealed himself
To Gonzalo first of all,
And calling him 'my dearest friend'
He asked him to recall...

How he had helped him to survive
A voyage filled with strife,
And said he was his truest friend
Because he'd saved his life.

Antonio and the chastened king
Both bowed down very low,
For now they saw before them
Ill-treated Prospero.

'Forgive me!' begged Antonio
On his knees – time after time;
The king said he was sorry for
Assisting with the crime.

So Prospero forgave them both,
He was a kindly man,
And they agreed that once again
He'd be Duke of Milan.

Then Prospero showed the king his son
Who, with Miranda there,
Was calmly playing chess, as if
They didn't have a care.

The king was quite bewildered
Though overcome with joy –
He scarcely could believe that here
He'd found his own dear boy.

They hugged each other saying,
'This surely cannot be.'
As each had thought the other was
Forever lost at sea.

The king was quite astonished by
Miranda's lovely face.
He said, 'Who is this beauteous maid
With charm and boundless grace?'

'This lady,' Ferdinand replied,
'So beautiful and fine,
Has smiled on me today and has
Consented to be mine.

'I could not ask your blessing
Because I thought you dead,
But now with your permission,
We would like to wed.

'And she is Prospero's daughter,
True ruler of Milan.
He'll be my second father,
A worthy, upright man.'

Then with emotion running high,
They each one hugged the other,
And Prospero again forgave
His wicked, erring brother.

Antonio was quite borne down
With shame and deep remorse.
Gonzalo wept outright to see
Events take such a course.

Prospero said, 'The ship is safe,
With all of those on board.'
Then offered them the finest meal
His island could afford.

He called on Caliban to serve
A lavish, tasty feast.
The company were all amazed
To see this monstrous beast.

Prospero called to Ariel:
'As you've been true to me,
I shall now keep my promise
And I will set you free.'

Then later Prospero buried
Within a hidden nook,
His trusty wand, his potions
And his great magic book.

He now resolved that he would make
A fresh, unfettered start,
Renouncing altogether
The practice of his art.

He would no longer cast his spells,
But be the duke again,
With no more thoughts of magic –
For he would now abstain.

Reunited with his brother
And also with the king,
His heart was full of gladness and
Took joy in everything.

And eager to return at last
Unto his native land,
He had the ship made ready for
This very happy band.

Ariel was so grateful now
To be completely free,
And as he watched the ship set sail
Across the deep, blue sea...

In gratitude to Prospero
For their time together,
He calmed the sea to make quite sure
The ship enjoyed fine weather!

*When he arrived, he should recount
The story of his life*

PERICLES, PRINCE OF TYRE

Pericles, the Prince of Tyre
Found something out one day
That gave him such an awful shock
He had to run away.

The secret he unearthed about
Antioch's great king
Was something really terrible;
A shocking, monstrous thing.

Whatever in the world was it
That caused the prince to run?
What dreadful thing had happened?
What had this bad king done?

Well he possessed a daughter –
A lovely looking girl;
She set the heart of everyone
Aflame and in a whirl.

Her beauty brought her suitors
From far and wide and so,
One day the youthful Pericles
Decided he would go…

To win the beauty for himself –
She'd make a lovely wife.
He knew, however, if he failed
Then he would lose his life.

Antiochus had set things up
In quite a cunning way,
For everyone who lost found out,
There was a price to pay.

To win his precious daughter's hand
A riddle must be solved.
Those who failed would meet their death,
No-one would be absolved.

But Pericles thought, 'I must try',
For she was quite a catch,
And everyone at court all thought
They'd make a lovely match.

So off he went to see the king
And meet his daughter too,
For he was quite determined
To see the project through.

They handed him a riddle;
'Solve it,' the vile king said,
'And you, my dear Prince Pericles,
Shall share my daughter's bed.'

So Pericles perused the words
And to his horror saw
That they concealed a wicked act
That was against the law.

Other suitors hadn't seen,
But Pericles — in a flash —
Discerned the meaning and it turned
His every hope to ash.

For though the riddle tried to hide
The answer, not impart
The very deed that it contained,
The wise prince — with a start...

Perceived that in it was revealed
Admission to a fact
That decent people all abhor,
A really awful act.

The king had practiced incest
With his young daughter there:
The whole affair was obvious,
They were a brazen pair.

The young prince was astounded,
His feelings ran amok!
He did his best to cover up
His horror and his shock.

So when he gave his answer
He spoke thus to disguise
The fact he'd worked the whole thing out —
He told a few white lies.

But the evil king could see
That this good-looking youth
Had in a moment understood
The foul and tawdry truth.

'He's worked it out,' he whispered,
'But I'll play with him awhile.
Please take more time to answer,'
He said with artful smile.

Pericles was much relieved
To gain a short respite,
For he'd been worried for his life
As truthfully he might.

He decided there and then
That he would have to flee.
'I'm getting out of here,' he thought,
'Before he murders me.'

And so he rushed off back to Tyre,
And on arriving there
He said to Helicanus:
'We all must need beware.

'Antiochus sleeps with his girl
And so I fear that Tyre
Will feel the wrath of this bad king –
We'll all be in the mire.

'For he's aware, I know full well,
That I have worked it out.'
He then told Helicanus
What it was all about.

Helicanus answered him,
He said, 'I've known you since
You were a boy – so heed me well:
You now must flee, my prince.

'Sail for Tarsus right away;
You must get out of here.'
Said Pericles, 'I'm sure you're right.
I must leave home, I fear.'

And so he sailed for Tarsus
Just in the nick of time.
The king of Antioch was keen
To cover up his crime,

So sent his servant Thaliard,
To murder Pericles:
But the prince had sailed away –
He'd caught the evening breeze.

When he arrived in Tarsus
He found a famine there;
The city was in dire distress,
With hunger everywhere.

But Pericles saw he could help
By sharing out his food.
This put the governor, Cleon,
Into a gracious mood.

'Thank you for your generous help;
I thank you for the bread,
And all the other tasty things,'
The grateful Cleon said.

And then from Helicanus
The prince received a note.
It counselled him to watch his back
And this is what he wrote:

'Antiochus has been informed,
He knows just where you stay.
Before he sends assassins –
You should be on your way.'

Once more with trepidation
Our hero, Pericles,
Takes a ship and sets his course
Across the deep, blue seas.

But then a tempest wracked the ship;
It tossed the craft around
Until it gave up fighting
And sank without a sound.

Everybody perished –
Except Prince Pericles;
He was washed up on a shore
Beneath some tall palm trees.

He walked along the lonely beach
And met three fishermen.
These lads were very kind to him
And told him there and then...

About the land to which he'd come –
Pentapolis its name.
Simonides was ruler there
And he enjoyed great fame...

For always being virtuous
And acting with such cheer;
All called him 'good' Simonides
And held him very dear.

His daughter was called Thaisa –
Perfect in every way,
And celebrations were arranged
Upon the following day...

To mark this daughter's birthday,
And tournaments would be
Fought by knights and princes –
At court for all to see.

The prince was keen to join the jousts
But had no armour there,
For it had all been lost at sea:
He felt a great despair.

He would have loved to join the fun
But he was in a hole,
For with no armour he could not
Assume an active role.

But then a fisherman came up
And said, 'Look what I've caught.'
It was the armour he had lost –
The very suit he sought.

And so next day he made his way
To court, so he could fight
With every brave, heroic prince,
And every valiant knight...

Who strove to gain the honour
Of lovely Thaisa's praise,
By daring deeds of bravery
To make her passions blaze.

Bold Pericles fought very well,
He was a raging sight,
In fact his courage was so great
That he won every fight.

Thaisa was quite overcome
And so with trembling knees,
Bestowed her royal favour
Upon brave Pericles.

In his triumphant moment,
The prince felt Cupid's dart,
And to the lovely Thaisa
He quickly lost his heart.

The princess too was smitten
By this bold, handsome lad,
So when he asked to marry her,
She turned to her dear dad…

With looks that very clearly told
Her father, she was hooked –
And with no more discussion
A wedding day was booked.

But Pericles was still afraid
Of Antioch's foul king,
So he did not divulge his rank;
He didn't say a thing.

~ ~ ~

Some months passed and then news came
Antiochus was dead,
So Pericles told Thaisa,
'It is a prince you've wed.'

Simonides was overjoyed:
He got in quite a state.
'My daughter's married to a prince —
Well, this is really great.'

Helicanus had sent news;
He'd said, 'Come right away,
'Twould be unwise, my dear, young prince
To tarry or delay.

'Your subjects are impatient,
They want your presence here;
If you do not return to Tyre,
There could be grief I fear.'

'I must go,' said Pericles;
Thaisa was with child —
So added, 'You remain right here,
The sea can be so wild...

'It would not be advisable
For you to make the trip;
We do not want you giving birth
While you're on board a ship.'

Thaisa wouldn't have it.
She said, 'I'll be okay.'
So Pericles agreed because
She always got her way.

And they set sail – but in no time
It began to rain,
And then a mighty storm ensued –
Such rotten luck again.

Thaisa shook with awful fear
For all that she was worth,
And then right there within the storm
The poor scared girl gave birth.

The nurse caught up the baby,
And as the infant cried,
Upon that tossing, storm-wracked ship,
Princess Thaisa died.

The nurse then took the baby girl
To Pericles and said,
'Here is your little girl, my lord;
Your dear wife, though, is dead.'

Pericles was overcome
With dreadful pain and grief.
However much he cried and railed
It gave him no relief.

And he cried out above the storm,
'Ye Gods! Why do you give
Such goodly gifts to mortals
And then not let them live?'

He took the baby girl and said,
'May your sweet life be mild,
For no child ever had a birth
More blustery or wild.

'For you have lost the person
More dear than any other;
I have lost a treasured wife,
And you a loving mother.'

The storm gave not the slightest sign
Of going to abate,
And a corpse on board a ship
Is something sailors hate.

For they were superstitious,
They felt they'd get no peace
And if the body stayed on board
The storm would never cease.

They came to Pericles and said,
'We must demand, my lord,
The corpse of your departed wife
Be thrown now overboard.

'It is the only way by which
The weather will transform;
It is the only way to stop
This monumental storm.'

Pericles was well aware
Their fears were quite unfounded;
But if he argued, knew for sure
That they would be astounded...

For superstition runs so deep
Within a sailor's creed:
Thus with sadness and remorse
Fraught Pericles agreed.

He went to see his Thaisa
One last and final time;
He gazed down on her lovely face,
So peaceful and sublime.

He said, 'My dear, beloved wife,
I beg you pardon me,
For I've been told that I must cast
Your body in the sea.'

The sailors brought a casket,
And placed the girl inside;
And as they did it, Pericles
Stood by and softly cried.

He laid some precious gems within
The casket, then he wrote
A message saying who she was,
And lastly, placed a note...

Beside his wife just lying there;
The note conveyed a plea:
'If she is found, please bury her.'
Then he cast her in the sea.

At last the storm abated;
The prince said with a sigh,
'Unless we reach the nearest port
My child will also die.

'She needs good nursing right away,
The little babe is frail,
So plot your course with speed I say –
To Tarsus we will sail.'

~ ~ ~

Thaisa's chest was thrown about
In remorseless motion;
A fragile and a helpless thing
On that vast, mighty ocean.

It rose and fell and whirled about
Amid the deafening roar,
Until it was, by mighty waves,
Deposited on shore.

And as the chest lay on the beach
It was discovered there,
By servants who then carried it
To Cerimon, with care.

He was a great physician,
He really was the best,
And gingerly he opened up
Thaisa's burial chest.

And there he saw the princess with
The jewels and the note –
The one you will remember
Her grieving husband wrote.

And then he looked upon her face,
Observing that the flesh
Did not seem dead and lifeless,
In fact it looked quite fresh.

Cerimon then scratched his head
And said, 'It seems to me
They acted somewhat hastily
Who cast you in the sea.'

Then turning to those gathered there
Upon that windy day,
He said, 'It seems amazing
But I am bound to say...

'I think that there may be a chance
The girl is still alive;
I think with careful nurturing
That she may well revive.

'And though it looks as if she's dead
As she lies softly there,
I think that all she needs is warmth
And some refreshing air.'

And then just like a miracle,
Amid the servant's cries,
Thaisa started breathing –
She opened up her eyes.

She'd never actually been dead,
But, by unhappy chance,
After giving birth had swooned
And gone into a trance.

'Wherever in the world am I?
What is this place?' she said.
Cerimon sought to explain
How all had thought her dead.

He showed the note that Pericles
Had written and then sighed,
'Everyone on board your ship
Believed that you had died.'

She read the note and then exclaimed,
In tones – oh, so forlorn,
'I have no recollection of
My baby being born.

'And as I'll never ever see
My Pericles again,
I'll enter a religious house
And there I will remain.'

Said Cerimon, 'If that's your wish
Then take good heart, my dear;
The Temple of Diana
Is situated here.

'You can become a priestess
And in the temple share
A life of contemplation,
A life of pious prayer.'

And that is what sad Thaisa did,
Though missing Pericles:
She spent her time in fervent prayer,
Hands clasped and on her knees.

~ ~ ~

Meanwhile despondent Pericles
Took back the little waif
To Tarsus and to Cleon where
He thought that she'd be safe.

He spoke to Dionyza, who
Was friendly Cleon's wife:
'This is my child, Marina;
Her mother lost her life.'

He told them of the dreadful storm
And with paternal pride,
Spoke of the babe Marina's birth
And how his Thaisa died.

And then he said to Cleon
And Dionyza too,
'I cannot raise the child myself,
I don't know what to do.

'So can I leave her in your care?
For I would much prefer
She's raised within a family.
Will you look after her?'

Cleon and his wife replied,
'Of course we will, my lord.
We will treat her as our own;
She shall be our ward.

'We owe you, prince, so very much,
For all the food you gave,
You saved the whole of Tarsus from
A grim, untimely grave.

'So we will raise her properly
And if we need a spur,
The whole of Tarsus will ensure
We take good care of her.'

So having sorted things this way,
And having thanked the pair,
Pericles returned to Tyre
And once more settled there.

~ ~ ~

Many years have now elapsed.
Marina has thus grown
Into a daughter any man
Would gladly call his own.

She had the sweetest singing voice
And, oh, how she could dance!
In everything she did she had
The power to entrance.

Soft hair fell on her shoulders,
She had a lovely face,
And every action that she took
Was carried out with grace.

So maybe it is no surprise
She roused some jealousy;
Most came from Dionyza,
As we shall quickly see.

For Cleon's wife had given birth
About the selfsame time,
That Thaisa bore Marina,
In that inclement clime.

Their poor daughter was quite slow,
Perhaps because her days
Were spent beneath the shadow of
Marina's constant praise.

Dionyza felt that if
Marina wasn't there
Her daughter would receive at once
Much more respect and care.

She wouldn't suffer every day
The gross indignity,
Of being made to feel that she
Was second best, you see.

She knew a very evil man,
One Leonine by name;
To have Marina murdered
Was Dionyza's aim.

But even wicked Leonine
Recoiled from such an act.
He said, 'She has such virtue —
All know this for a fact.'

'Then this is all more reason,'
Foul Dionyza said,
'Why the gods should have her,
Why she should be dead.'

Leonine spoke softly:
'It is my job to kill,
And so your faithful servant
Will go and do your will.'

And as he spoke Marina
Came walking by that way;
She was in mourning for her nurse
Who'd sadly died that day.

'Let Leonine go with you,'
Her jealous guardian sighed,
'For he is just as sad as you
That your poor nurse has died.'

Marina wished to be alone
And she at first resisted,
But Dionyza spoke again
And firmly she insisted.

So the two set off at once
And walked along the shore;
Marina had no inkling
Of what might lie in store.

But Leonine then up and said,
'My dear young lady fair,
I bid you now be silent
For you must say a prayer.'

'What do you mean?' Marina asked,
'Why have you brought me here?'
And then the poor girl realised
She had good cause to fear.

'Now say your prayer,' the man replied,
'There is no time to waste,
For I am sworn to do my work
Both cleanly and with haste.

'You do not need a lot of time
To pray – for what I hear
Is that the gods know everything
And they are quick of ear.'

'Do you intend to kill me?'
The hapless creature said.
'Why in the world should you require
To see this poor maid dead?'

'My mistress wills it,' he replied.
'I'm sorry you must die.'
'I've never caused offence,' she said.
'I've never hurt a fly.

'Why does she want to kill me?
Why ever must I bleed?'
He said, 'Mine's not to reason why
But just to do the deed.'

But at the very moment
That he drew out his knife
In awful preparation
To take the poor girl's life...

Pirates landed on the shore –
And, right before the eyes
Of Leonine, they carried off
Marina as their prize.

They took the girl to Mytilene
And on arriving there
They sold her to a brothel,
Much to her despair.

But she was most determined
That she would stay quite chaste,
And she was fiery in the way
She showed her great distaste.

So when the brothel owner
Sent clients to the maid,
She preached to them of virtue
In order to dissuade...

These men from their intentions.
She made them feel ashamed –
And so they always went away,
Their passions duly tamed.

And then she even managed to
Convert the brothel boss.
He wasn't very happy –
In fact he was quite cross,

But he saw there was no way
That he would stand a chance
Of changing her – so he agreed
She could teach song and dance...

And show the others how to weave
And also how to sew;
And thus she kept her honour
Intact and all aglow...

With not a stain upon it;
Her standards high and strong,
So everybody clearly saw
That she would do no wrong.

~ ~ ~

Back in Tyre, Prince Pericles
Decided he would go
To Tarsus – for he thought it time
For him to get to know...

His daughter, whom he'd sadly left
So many years before.
He was most anxious now to see
His little girl once more.

Helicanus went with him,
To keep him company,
So once again Prince Pericles
Set out across the sea.

When he arrived he heard the news
His daughter was now dead.
'We put up this fine monument,'
Sly Dionyza said.

She really thought she told the truth;
She *thought* the girl had died,
For Leonine had told her this,
But then, of course, he'd lied.

Poor Pericles felt desperate.
With tears and trembling lip,
He rushed away from Cleon's court
And went aboard his ship...

Set sail at once, and in good time,
Arrived in Mytilene,
Which, of course, is where we know
Marina to have been.

The governor of Mytilene
Put on his Sunday best,
Then boarding his official barge
Went out to meet his guest.

But when he said, 'I'm here to greet
This visitor who's come...'
Lord Helicanus sadly said,
'My master's very glum.

'He will not speak to anyone –
So let me keep it brief:
He's lost his wife and daughter so
He's quite consumed with grief.'

The governor, Lysimachus,
Said, 'Well now, here's a plan –
A way, I think, that we could help
To cheer up this sad man.'

He thought that sweet Marina
Could really help a lot;
He knew her well and in his heart
He held a tender spot.

And so he sent Marina,
Although still very young,
To talk to this Prince Pericles,
For she was sweet of tongue.

If anyone could ease his pain
He thought Marina could,
For she was known by everyone
To be extremely good.

She went to see sad Pericles,
And when he heard her speak
He sat up slightly in his chair –
Things did not look so bleak.

Then when he saw the girl's sweet face,
He thought, 'Upon my life,
She is the spitting image of
My poor long lost dear wife.'

He started asking questions.
'Tell me your tale,' he said.
Marina then began to speak
About the life she'd led.

She told him she was born at sea
And how her mother died;
How she was left at Tarsus –
Poor Pericles then cried;

For he now saw before him
The girl whom he'd been told
Was buried and forgotten,
Her body long since cold.

But here she was alive and well,
His little baby girl;
It made his mixed emotions
Erupt into a whirl.

He embraced his daughter;
Marina hugged him too.
He told her how he loved her;
She said, 'And I love you.'

But all of this excitement
Made Pericles feel strained;
I guess it's little wonder that
The poor man was quite drained.

He fell into a happy sleep
With many a heartfelt sigh,
And as he slept, Marina,
Sat lovingly close by.

And deep in sleep he had a dream
That he must go with haste
Unto Diana's temple –
There was no time to waste.

When he arrived he should recount
The story of his life:
All his great misfortunes
And how he lost his wife.

So Pericles and his dear child
Made their weary way
Unto Diana's temple,
Intending there to pray.

But as they entered, standing there
Was Cerimon – the chap
Whose skill had raised poor Thaisa from
Her cold and deathlike nap.

And standing to one side of him
Was dearest Thaisa too,
And when she saw Prince Pericles
She absolutely knew...

It was her long lost husband.
She listened as he spoke,
And every word he uttered
Made Princess Thaisa choke.

He spoke about his dear dead wife –
He broke down for a while –
Then spoke about Marina
And all about her trial.

Thaisa was quite overcome,
And she could bear no more.
She cried, 'Oh royal Pericles!'
Then fainted on the floor.

Pericles was most surprised,
He shouted, 'What's amiss?
Who is this fainting woman
And what means all of this?'

Cerimon addressed the prince:
'Sir, listen well to me.
This poor lady is the one
You threw into the sea.

'You thought that on that dreadful day
Your wife had lost her life,
But I revived her with my skill –
This lady *is* your wife.'

Pericles was overjoyed
And with no further qualms
He said, 'Be buried once again
Within my loving arms.'

Pericles then told her,
'Here is your daughter fair.'
Thaisa was quite overcome
To see Marina there.

And then in front of everyone
The prince said that he thought,
The governor – Lysimachus –
And his dear girl should court.

They'd make a lovely couple,
And then the young pair said
They truly liked each other
And would be pleased to wed.

Now there is only one thing left
That it remains to tell:
Of Cleon and his wicked wife
And what to them befell.

The kindly folk of Tarsus, when
They learned of what they'd done,
Went wild with righteous anger
And all rose up as one.

They burned the royal palace –
The pair of them inside.
The desperate couple cowered there.
They had nowhere to hide.

And so they died an awful death,
Alone, without a friend;
And thus for them it really was
A truly awful end.

Pericles told Thaisa,
'Your father is now dead,
So thus in Pentapolis
We will now reign instead.'

She was most distraught to learn
Simonides had died,
But she was reassured to have
Pericles by her side.

And then the prince continued –
He gave a new decree;
He planned to send his daughter,
To Tyre – across the sea.

He said, 'Lysimachus, now take
Marina, your new bride
To Tyre and be the ruler there –
My daughter at your side.'

So these two noble heroes
Wore their respective crowns –
A satisfactory outcome
From all the ups and downs.

He gathered up the little girl

THE WINTER'S TALE

Leontes, King of Sicily,
And Hermione, his queen,
Enjoyed a life as happy
As any ever seen.

But Leontes sometimes said,
'Although our life is sweet,
I can't deny I sometimes feel
That I would like to meet...

'My dear old friend, Polixenes,
And chat with him a while,
For out of all the friends I've had
He stood out by a mile.'

He'd often tell Hermione,
'My friend was such a brick,
To have you meet Polixenes
Would give me such a kick.'

You see, these two devoted friends
Attended the same school,
But then Leontes had returned
To Sicily to rule.

His father had died suddenly,
So this had put in train
A sequence of events that meant
He'd gone back home to reign.

His friend, Polixenes, as well
Had suffered a sad loss;
His father too had passed away,
So he became the boss...

Of beautiful Bohemia –
Took over from his dad;
He became the country's king
Although still but a lad.

So these two close and faithful friends,
With tears in their eyes
Had fondly and reluctantly
Exchanged their last goodbyes.

Though they'd been close since childhood,
They went their separate ways,
Destined now to live apart
For their remaining days.

They sent each other letters though,
Which always gave a lift;
At Christmas and on birthdays
They'd always send a gift.

And so the years went by, it seemed
They'd never meet again,
Because it takes great effort
To rule a state and reign.

Leontes often sent a note
To his much missed old chum;
He'd say, 'I wish you'd visit,
I really wish you'd come.

'Please join me here in Sicily –
We'll have a great old time.
To get together once again
Would really be sublime.'

At last Polixenes gave in
To these repeated pleas –
When Leontes wrote and said,
'I'm begging on my knees.'

He couldn't find the words to say
No, to this request,
And so he wrote confirming
He'd come to be his guest.

At first the visit was great fun,
For it was nothing less
Than triumph – quite momentous –
A really great success.

They talked about the times they'd shared
When each had been a child;
About the pranks and scrapes and fun
And all their running wild.

They told Hermione everything,
And she, with merry heart,
Joined in their boyish happiness
And took a cheerful part...

In all their conversation;
It was tremendous fun,
Until the day Polixenes
Declared the trip was done.

'I must go home,' he said at last,
'I've been away too long.'
Leontes said, 'Another month
Would surely do no wrong.'

He tried his best to make his friend
Remain a longer while.
'Alas!' Polixenes replied,
Though with a winning smile...

'I really must be going,
I should be getting back,
I've got a kingdom there to run –
And kings must not be slack.'

Hermione, with honeyed words
And her persuasive way,
Said, 'Dear Polixenes, my friend
Please linger here, I pray.

Stay just a little longer;
We love your company.'
Enraptured, good Polixenes
Obeyed her fervent plea.

He said, 'All right, my firm resolve
You cleverly have turned.'
And though it seemed a joyous thing,
A jealousy now burned...

Within Leontes' manly heart –
'Twas envy of a kind
So keen, so deep and dangerous,
It fairly turned his mind.

He thought that something was amiss:
His friend had told him, 'No!'
When he had pleaded desperately
And begged him not to go.

But one word from Hermione –
'Oh, please don't go away' –
Sufficed at once to change his mind,
And now he said he'd stay.

Although Hermione had won
Her husband's great desire,
Leontes thought each word she said
Implied she was a liar.

He also then began to think
His erstwhile loyal friend,
Was after his Hermione –
This was his selfish end...

To try and take her from him –
Of course he was quite wrong;
His wife was true and faithful
To Leontes all along.

His anger and his jealousy
Both bound him in a knot;
He turned into a monster –
He really lost the plot.

He sent for Lord Camillo
And told him of his pain,
He said, 'My friend is ruining
My marriage, that is plain.

"There's something shifty going on,
I want it stopped right now.'
'Tell me your wish,' Camillo said
And gave a courtier's bow.

'Give poison to Polixenes –
I want it done today.
He's made me very angry,
I want him out the way!'

Camillo was a decent sort,
And though Leontes sounded
So certain – Lord Camillo knew
His envy was unfounded.

He knew that Queen Hermione
Was no unfaithful wife;
On this he would have gladly staked
His highly valued life.

Camillo told Polixenes
Just what the king had said;
How he desired him poisoned –
How he wished him dead.

Astounded, King Polixenes
Was very grateful too.
He said, 'My dear Camillo
I owe great thanks to you.'

Polixenes escaped at once;
He fled away that night.
Camillo went along as well –
The pair slipped out of sight.

Once safely in Bohemia
A friendship grew between
Camillo and Polixenes,
As close as it had been…

Between Leontes and the king –
Though that was in the past.
It seemed that some firm friendships
Are destined not to last!

~ ~ ~

The news of their escape had put
Leontes in a rage.
He stormed about the palace –
He didn't act his age.

His fury overwhelmed him
And overcome with gloom,
At last he sought Hermione
Within her private room.

She was with Mamillius,
Their son, when he burst in.
He told his wife that she had lied,
Committed carnal sin.

Hermione was pregnant, but
He said, 'Your child's not mine,
The father is Polixenes,
That so-called friend's a swine!'

He raged and carried on so much
Mamillius got upset;
Leontes wasn't worried though,
He wasn't finished yet.

He just ignored his crying son
No matter how he wailed,
And turning to his wife he said,
'You're going to be jailed.'

And that is what Leontes did –
He threw his wife in jail;
And then he summoned two great lords
And told them to set sail...

Towards Apollo's sacred shrine
At Delphi and, once there,
To ask the Oracle if his wife
Was having an affair.

And so the Lord Cleomenes
And good Lord Dion too
Both hastened to the Oracle,
As the king had bid them do.

~ ~ ~

Meanwhile poor Hermione,
Innocent of the crime
For which she'd been imprisoned,
Was having a bad time.

She languished in her dismal cell
Though she had done no wrong.
But then a baby girl was born:
A daughter came along.

She looked down on the lovely child,
So sweet and all brand new,
And said, 'Poor little prisoner,
I'm innocent like you.'

The queen's best friend, Paulina,
Was visiting the jail
To see how she was feeling.
Her maid said, 'She's still frail.'

Paulina said, 'Although the king
Is acting very wild,
I still feel totally convinced
That he should see this child.'

Emilia, the maid agreed.
'One look and we may find
The sight of such a bonny girl
Will help to change his mind.'

Paulina said, 'Then ask the queen
If she will trust in me
And let me take the baby,
Just so the king can see...

'The pretty little girl he has –
It's bound to change his view –
And he'll embrace his daughter then,
And free Hermione too.'

Emilia very soon returned
With smiles upon her face,
And in her arms she held the girl,
Wrapped in the finest lace.

She said, 'The queen's delighted;
She thought no-one would dare
To take her daughter to the king
But bids you to beware.

'He's in an awful temper,
As I believe you know,
So pick your words most gingerly –
Be careful how you go.'

Paulina said of course she would,
Then took the baby girl.
She said, 'How could the king reject
This priceless little pearl?'

She forced her way into the king
And said, 'I do entreat
You look upon your daughter, sire.'
Then laid her at his feet.

'Have mercy on your little girl
And on your wife as well.'
But sadly all the king would do
Was stamp his feet and yell.

'Get out of here at once,' he cried.
He called Paulina's spouse.
'Antigonus, go take your wife
Out of my royal house.'

Antigonus removed his wife,
Paulina left the room,
But left the baby with the king,
Alone to face her doom.

Paulina hoped Leontes would,
Despite his angry passion,
Become enchanted by the child
And show her some compassion.

But she was wrong for now he called,
'Antigonus, come to me!
Go take this child and carry her
A long way out to sea.

'I do not want her presence here
For a moment more.
Find a distant, lonely place
And leave her on the shore.

'And there this child can perish;
Just leave her there to die.'
Antigonus picked up the girl
And said, 'You can rely...

'Upon your wishes being done,
My lord, I'll do the deed.
Don't be concerned a moment more –
I'll do it with all speed.'

~ ~ ~

And when Antigonus had gone
The king arranged a trial
For much maligned Hermione.
He'd hear of no denial.

He was impatient that her guilt
Be clear for all to see.
He said, 'Word from the Oracle
Will not discourage me.

'I know my wife is guilty;
It's time that she was taught
A lesson, so without delay
I'll bring her to the court.'

Hermione stood there trembling,
Her thoughts all in a whirl,
And she was also grieving
For her dear baby girl.

Then as the trial got underway
Two men walked through the door:
'Twas Dion and Cleomenes
That everyone now saw.

A message from the Oracle
They brought, for it had spoken.
Leontes gave stern orders,
The seal should now be broken.

'Read what the Oracle has said,
Do so without delay.'
The Oracle was opened up –
Here's what it had to say.

'Hermione is innocent;
Polixenes – no blame;
Camillo is a decent man;
The king now bears the name...

'Of wicked tyrant, one whose words
And actions are unfair;
Leontes bears the dreadful curse
Of life without an heir...

'Till that which is now lost be found;
This is my final word.'
The whole court gasped in horror
At what they had just heard.

Leontes would not heed these words,
He thought them merely lies,
Although the ancient Oracle
Was reckoned to be wise.

Then news of further tragedy
Arrived, which was the worst:
Hermione, on hearing it
Felt that her heart would burst.

For when Mamillius had been told,
'Your mother's being tried.'
He'd felt such grief and awful shame
That he'd collapsed and died.

Hermione fainted on the floor
In front of all the court.
The king in desperate sorrow cried,
Now totally distraught.

He told Paulina, 'Take the queen
And care for her, I pray.'
It was the last thing in the world
The court thought he would say.

With pity he was overcome
For his unhappy queen;
Maybe she was blameless;
Maybe she'd always been.

But as he thought these guilty thoughts
Paulina came and said,
'Hermione's heart has broken,
I fear, my king, she's dead!'

Leontes then collapsed and cried;
His soul was torn apart.
He saw that his ill usage had
Destroyed her loving heart.

He was repentant and distraught
For the way he'd been;
He vowed he'd mourn for evermore
His daughter, son and queen.

Then he recalled the Oracle –
Its words filled him with dread.
'Till that which is now lost be found,
You'll have no heir,' it said.

Now Mamillius was no more
That meant he had no heir,
Unless his daughter was brought back
And safely to his care.

~ ~ ~

But what of bold Antigonus?
Well, he'd set out to sea
With very little baggage and
The princess on his knee.

And yet this happy picture
Gives the wrong impression:
It seems to show he loved the child
He held in his possession.

But he was set upon a plan
To leave the child to die;
He'd do the deed the king required,
He would not reason why.

The ship was battered by a storm
And how the wind did roar,
Until the vessel came to land
Upon Bohemia's shore.

This was Polixenes's state,
And once the ship was safe,
Antigonus set down the child
And there he left the waif...

Alone upon the sandy shore
Where she was sure to die;
A prey to any hungry beast
That chanced to wander by.

And yet poetic justice
Was surely working there:
Antigonus, as he walked back,
Was eaten by a bear!

It caught him as he made his way
Back to the waiting ship;
He really didn't stand a chance
When once it got a grip.

As for the little princess,
Well she was quickly found;
A passing shepherd saw her as
She lay upon the ground.

She wore expensive clothes and jewels,
So it was very clear
She came of noble parentage,
But how did she get here?

The shepherd saw a message
Pinned to the baby's coat;
It was the child's name written there –
'Perdita' read the note.

He gathered up the little girl
And thus he saved her life,
And then with tender loving care
He took her to his wife.

They realised that all the jewels
Could change their life for sure;
With this new wealth they'd have no need
To struggle anymore.

But to conceal this treasure trove
They moved away that day
And started on another life
Some many miles away.

They bought a lot of sheep and soon
Their wealth began to grow.
They raised Perdita as their child
But never let her know...

How she'd been found upon the beach,
Abandoned – all alone.
They showered her with all their love
And raised her as their own.

One noble thing the shepherd did,
One thing he firmly said:
He vowed he'd save some of the jewels
For when the girl was wed.

~ ~ ~

And so the years passed slowly by
And young Perdita grew
Into a lovely daughter –
A good girl, through and through.

Polixenes possessed a son,
One Florizel by name.
This prince was hunting one hot day –
He was in search of game...

When riding by the shepherd's hut,
He suddenly espied
A maid so fair and lovely –
It made him break his ride.

This was of course, Perdita –
Her beauty stole his heart;
It only took a moment
And Cupid shot his dart.

Using the name of Doricles
Prince Florizel became
A frequent, ardent visitor
Disguised by this false name.

The king, his father, soon found out
Just what the lad was doing;
He wasn't pleased to find his son
Had now gone out a-wooing...

A lowly shepherd's daughter,
With such a common touch;
For him to love a peasant,
This really was too much.

He summoned Lord Camillo,
'You'll never guess,' he said,
'What Florizel is up to –
He must be off his head.

'He's seeing a poor shepherd girl
And spinning me some lies.
There's only one thing for it –
We must go in disguise...

'Unto the shepherd's dwelling
And spy on him awhile.
I find his liking for this girl
Contemptuous and vile.

'It really isn't fitting for
The offspring of a king
To lavish his affection so
On such a common thing.'

So Lord Camillo and the king
Sought out the shepherd's dwelling.
Within the king a mighty surge
Of anger was now swelling.

They approached the little hut
And as they both were nearing,
They heard a feast in progress there,
A party for sheep shearing.

They both were made most welcome
And took a seat inside,
And when Polixenes looked round
He instantly espied...

His dear, beloved Florizel.
The lad sat in a chair,
Hid in a shady corner and
The shepherd girl was there.

Polixenes approached the two
And to his son he said,
'Your mind is not on feasting,
Love thoughts are in your head.

'Your mind is on this lady, but
The pedlar's left, my boy,
And you have bought no trinkets –
You bought your love no toy.'

Florizel had no idea
That he addressed his dad;
He just surmised the old man thought
He was a lovelorn lad.

He said, 'My dearest love, right here,
Is really much too smart.
She doesn't want cheap fripperies –
She wants what's in my heart.

'And, as old man, you seem to know –
Or maybe you just guess –
What animates a lover's heart,
Please hear what I profess...

'That I will marry this dear girl,
I'll take her for my wife,
And with this solemn promise
I give myself for life.'

Polixenes went crazy then,
And ripped off his disguise.
His face was red and steaming
And anger filled his eyes.

'Young sir,' he cried with venom,
'You silly little fool!
How can you dare to speak like this?'
He really lost his cool.

'To marry such a low-born maid,
A worthless piece of tat,
A humble peasant with no class,
A scrounging shepherd's brat.

'If you see her again, I swear
Upon my dying breath,
I'll have her and her father here
Both cruelly put to death.'

This was very hard indeed;
The good prince was bereft.
The king gave orders that his son
Should follow him, then left.

Perdita there was horrified;
She thought she'd lost her beau –
For after what his dad had said
He wouldn't want to know.

She really felt their love was doomed –
This was her lovelorn view,
For surely what the king desired
Is what the prince would do.

But this, of course, was not the case.
The prince refused to go,
He wouldn't leave for all the world,
Because he loved her so.

But then Camillo, kind of heart,
Who thought the girl had style,
Said, 'You must both get far away
And then lie low awhile.

'I have a plan to help you both,
And this is now my thought;
The three of us will cross the sea
To Sicily's great court.

'Leontes will protect you
And keep you safe and sound,
Until Polixenes shall change
His point of view around –

'And says that he will let you wed;
And so do you agree?
Are both of you determined now
To come along with me?'

The lovers both agreed at once –
It was the thing to do.
Camillo asked the shepherd next,
'Will you come with us too?'

The shepherd said of course he would,
And took the things he'd found
On Perdita, as she'd lain
Abandoned on the ground.

He took the baby clothes and jewels
And also took the note;
The one that had been pinned upon
Her little overcoat.

Camillo for his part was pleased
To have the chance to see
His loved and very dearly missed
Home in Sicily.

For years before he'd been in touch
With Leontes so,
He knew that it would be quite safe
For all of them to go.

~ ~ ~

And so they sailed for Sicily
And on arriving there
They found Leontes mourning for
The son who'd been his heir.

He grieved for poor Mamillius
And it is true to tell
His wife and baby girl were both
Close to his thoughts as well.

But pleased to see Camillo back,
He grasped his hand and said,
'Oh welcome home my dear, old friend,
I feared you might be dead.'

He turned to Florizel and cried,
'You're welcome to my court.'
But when he saw Perdita there
He had a startling thought...

That she looked like Hermione.
He cried, 'You're like my queen!
I'm sure that this is just the way
My daughter would have been,

'If I had not destroyed her
By actions so inept;
I've lost her now forever.'
And he broke down and wept.

Then turning to Prince Florizel
He said to the young lad,
'I miss your father's friendship –
I really miss your dad.'

But through all this Leontes
Stayed constant to one thing:
He kept his gaze on Perdita –
A very troubled king.

He told them all the story, how
He'd sent his girl away.
The shepherd thought, 'It's his *princess*
I found that fateful day.'

He showed the king the garments and
The note that he had found,
And all the other items left
Around her on the ground.

He told the king just where she'd been.
He said, 'I saw her there,
Left by a man who, afterwards,
Was eaten by a bear.'

Paulina checked the writing in
The note and then she said,
'Antigonus has written this,
So he is surely dead.'

She grieved to hear the details of
Her husband's grisly slaughter,
But despite this news, rejoiced
The king had found his daughter.

But when Leontes realised
Perdita was his child,
Great sorrow swept across him –
His feelings drove him wild.

For though he was delighted
To find his girl again,
Now thinking of Hermione
He almost went insane.

He cried, 'Oh your dear mother,
If only she were here...
I treated her appallingly,
I've done great wrong, I fear.'

Paulina then spoke up and said,
'A statue at my house,
Is the spitting image of
Hermione, your spouse.

'It's only just been finished,
It really must be seen,
For it's the very image of
Your late, lamented queen.'

Leontes said he'd like to go;
Perdita too was keen
To see her mother's image
And look upon this queen.

For though 'twas but a statue
Made out of lifeless stone,
It was the closest she would get
To one she'd never known.

They went to good Paulina's house,
Where she drew back a screen,
And there before them they all saw
A statue of the queen.

Leontes didn't say a word,
He stood dumbstruck with awe;
He really was quite overcome
By everything he saw.

The statue was quite beautiful:
Hermione – nothing less.
It stood there, all resplendent
And in her finest dress.

'Is that not like your lovely queen?'
Paulina softly said.
The king replied, 'She stood like this
The day that we were wed.

'And yet she looked much younger then –
This statue makes her aged.'
Paulina said, 'The sculptor
With greatest skill has gauged...

'How fair Hermione would now look,
Were she alive today –
But let me now replace the screen
Lest you are moved to say...

'The statue is alive and breathes,
That you detect some motion,
That you persuade yourself she lives
Through your supreme devotion.'

The king cried out, 'Oh, were it true,
This surely would be bliss,
But please do not make fun of me
If I now place a kiss...

'Upon this gracious monument.
Perhaps she will revive...
To me she almost seems to breathe,
She seems to be alive.'

Perdita knelt upon the floor
With long and steady gaze;
The image of her mother had
The power to amaze.

She said, 'I could forever look
Upon my mother dear.
I only wish I'd known her well,
Not this cold statue here.'

Paulina said, 'My gracious lord,
If you will now approve,
And not say I have wicked powers,
I'll make the statue move.'

'Do what you will,' the king replied,
For he was quite astonished.
'I shall believe it when I see,'
He quietly admonished.

Paulina ordered music;
As it began to play,
The statue drew a heavy breath
And then began to sway.

It stepped down from the pedestal,
The most amazing thing;
Then with a smile upon its face
Embraced the startled king.

It truly *was* Hermione,
She wasn't really dead.
She prayed for blessings to come down
Upon her husband's head,

And on her daughter, Perdita.
Oh, what a sight to see;
The courtiers beholding this
Were happy as could be.

Hermione had made pretence
That she had sadly died,
So when Paulina gave this news –
She'd very boldly lied.

But now the queen had been restored
Unto the king again,
There's very little of our tale
Remaining to explain.

Leontes and Hermione
Called Florizel their son;
They said they were most grateful
For all the prince had done.

For he had loved their daughter when
She seemed of common stock;
But as they said these kindly words
They got another shock.

Polixenes himself walked in,
Looking for his boy.
When Leontes saw his friend
He almost jumped for joy.

The friends were quickly reconciled.
Polixenes agreed
That Florizel could marry –
He'd no longer have to plead.

For Perdita was nobly born
And not a 'shepherd's brat!'
So everyone lived happily
And that, at last, was that.

With no more false suspicions –
No more unhappy tears,
And all the people in this tale
Lived on for many years.

The youths are stuck in jail

THE TWO NOBLE KINSMEN

The Duke of Athens, Theseus,
Got in a fight one day,
To right a wrong and he was set
To boldly have his way.

He fought the court of ancient Thebes;
It was a raging sight –
But after many twists and turns
Brave Theseus won the fight.

He took some captives home with him,
He took them as his prize,
And in amongst them were a pair
Of cousins – two young guys.

Their uncle was King Creon;
In Thebes he was the boss.
These princes were a mite upset,
Fed up and very cross.

They hated being prisoners,
They cursed and swore out loud
For being royal princes,
They both were very proud.

So this is where our tale begins:
The youths are stuck in jail.
The prison's grim, the walls are thick,
The air is very stale.

But Palamon at length declares,
'Arcite, my dear friend,
I do not think that anything
Could make our friendship end...

'For we are really quite as close
As two good friends could be.'
Arcite smiled, 'My cousin dear,
I readily agree.'

Then Palamon, on looking down
Between the prison bars,
Beheld a sight more beautiful
Than heaven's brightest stars.

For in a garden far below,
There walked Emilia fair,
And when he saw her, Palamon
Could only stop and stare.

She won his heart the instant that
He saw her from above.
He knew she was the one for him –
The prince was deep in love.

Emilia was the sister to
The Duke of Athens' bride;
She'd come to join her sister,
To be right by her side.

As Palamon stood there transfixed,
Amazement on his face,
Arcite said, 'Let's have a look.
Move over – make some space.'

He too looked down from way above,
And when he saw the girl
Her beauty also won his heart;
His feelings were awhirl.

She was the prettiest creature
His eyes had ever seen,
For she was gentle, fair of face,
Most gracious and serene.

She looked so small and dainty as
She walked there on her own;
Arcite, in that moment vowed,
'She will be mine alone.'

But Palamon was quick to say –
His heart was fit to burst –
'She's mine, for it was I who saw
This lovely lady first.'

'That doesn't mean a thing at all,'
Arcite then cried out.
Palamon then yelled as well –
They both began to shout.

And in a moment all was changed:
From being friends they were
Reduced to calling names – such as
'You dog! You fiend! You cur!'

They argued then most angrily
Within their little cell.
These former friends gave each to each
All kinds of verbal hell.

But then the jailor came to say
The duke desired to speak
To Arcite, who thought things now
Had gone from bad to bleak.

He felt it meant more trouble,
So he was filled with fear,
But he did not expect to learn
What he was set to hear.

The duke said, 'You can go at once.
Get out of Athens now.
But if we find you here again,
One thing I firmly vow...

'That it will be the worst for you.
Now my young prince – depart!'
So Arcite then turned to leave
With very heavy heart...

For he now left Emilia –
He didn't want to go.
He envied Palamon so much –
He saw him as a foe.

For Palamon could see the girl,
The object of their love,
By gazing from the window there,
Which looked down from above.

Arcite vowed right there and then,
'I'd much prefer to be
In Palamon's grim prison cell
Than be outside and free.'

So, feeling in this way, I guess
It comes as no surprise,
Arcite thought that he'd return
But dressed in a disguise.

He met some folk along the road,
All going to a fair –
One organised by Theseus.
He thought, 'I'll join them there.'

So in disguise, he made his way
Straight back to Athens, then
He joined in all the sporting trials
Against the strongest men.

He entered each event and thus
He took on everyone,
And he came out on top each time –
Yes, every time he won.

Theseus was so impressed,
He thought, 'This lad's a star.
He's really quite exceptional,
The very best by far.

'So he deserves a special place
Within my service here.'
He gave Arcite then a post
That made the young prince cheer.

He was appointed servant to
His own true heart's desire:
Emilia – his one true love –
Who'd set his heart on fire.

~ ~ ~

But what of young Prince Palamon
Within that jail so grim?
How has *he* been getting on?
What's happening to him?

Well, he has had a bit of luck:
The jailor's daughter there
Has told him that she loves him so
And that it isn't fair...

That he's imprisoned and she says,
'My darling, do not fear.
I'll find you food and clothing,
Then get you out of here.'

And she was faithful to her word –
She got the poor chap out
By taking full advantage of
A jailor's daughter's clout.

~ ~ ~

The fair was still progressing –
Arcite felt such joy
To be there with Emilia
And serve in her employ.

But then one day he felt a shove,
Someone gave him a push,
And turning he saw Palamon
Emerging from a bush.

He still was locked in shackles –
A prisoner on the run –
While his cousin, Arcite,
Was there just having fun.

It only took a moment
Before they both grew rude,
And, yelling at each other then,
Renewed their angry feud.

They shouted out and ranted
Till they were out of breath,
And then agreed that they would fight
Each other to the death.

It seemed to them the only way
To settle their dispute,
For it would leave one man alone
To prosecute his suit.

Arcite said, 'Before we fight
You must consume some food,
And we must get those shackles off –
They'll hinder and protrude.

'For if we are to fight we must
Ensure the fight is fair.'
Although their course was set they were
A very courteous pair.

So later on when all was done,
They then prepared to fight,
And, of course, each prince believed
That he was in the right.

But when they donned their armour
Each one was pleasant to
The other as they kindly asked,
'Can I give help to you?

'And please say if your mail's too tight.
And are your gloves okay?
And if your armour's chafing –
Don't hesitate to say.'

Then finally they both were set,
Each ready for a fight;
But then as if from nowhere,
The duke came into sight.

He and his court were hunting.
'What's going on?' he cried.
The two young princes both spoke out.
You'd think they would have lied,

But they told Theseus the truth;
They told him who they were.
'We're fighting for Emilia,
We're both in love with her.'

The duke was very angry,
His face turned brightest red.
'I sentence both of you to die,'
He most severely said.

Emilia, who was standing there,
Gasped in distress and sighed.
'Oh please don't kill them. Banish them –
Oh please, my lord,' she cried.

But Theseus then turned and spoke
Some words he thought were wise:
A smart solution, so he thought,
Which gave her a surprise.

'I'll tell you what we'll do,' he said.
'They're young and should have wives,
And you are also young and wish
To save these princes' lives.

'So I propose that you should take
One of these fellows here
To be your partner.' She replied,
'I cannot choose, I fear.

'For they are both so excellent,
It would be hard to voice
A preference – I really can't
Begin to make a choice'

So Theseus spoke out again:
'We'll settle this my way.
You'll both return to Athens in
Just one month from today,

'And you will fight a duel here.
The winner,' he then said,
'Will marry fair Emilia –
The other lose his head!'

~ ~ ~

A month passed by and all alone –
Within her palace room –
Emilia gazed at pictures
Of the princes, both of whom...

She held in high affection.
They each displayed such grace;
And both of them were manly,
And oh so fine of face.

But now the princes have returned;
Emilia kneels and prays.
'Please let the winner be the one
Who loves me best,' she says.

She cannot stand to watch the fight,
But still retains her poise
As to her anxious ears is brought
The din and clashing noise...

As mighty sword strikes mighty sword,
As mace pounds on a shield –
And from the tumult it is clear
That neither prince will yield.

But then she hears a lusty shout.
So who has won the fight?
She thinks that Palamon has won,
But finds she isn't right.

Arcite comes before her
And bows down very low.
He says, 'Sweet lady, I now claim
The right to be your beau.'

But as he celebrates the fact
That he has won her love,
Poor Palamon is on his knees
In prayer to heaven above.

For he is now about to die,
He is about to feel
The axeman's blade across his neck;
This was, we know, the deal.

And though Emilia pleaded hard
With every single breath,
The Duke of Athens said that nought
Could save him now from death.

And so the valiant Palamon,
Bravely, but in shock,
Is led to execution –
To face the axeman's block.

He holds himself erect and tall,
Determined that he'll die
Like one who's born of royal blood.
He looks up to the sky...

And thus surveys the scudding clouds
As they pass high above,
And then his mind is filled with thoughts
Of his dear now lost love.

He says a heartfelt prayer, and then
With but a little sigh,
He says, 'My dear Emilia,
I bid you now goodbye.

'I lost you in fair fight – you'll not
Now live life by my side,
And as I die, I must accept
You'll be my cousin's bride.'

But at that very moment
As he prepares to die,
When he has made his final prayer,
He hears a garbled cry.

A messenger has come with news.
The man cries in remorse:
'Arcite has been injured,
He's fallen from his horse.'

And so brave Palamon is spared.
He goes to his old friend,
And there it is he witnesses
Arcite's dismal end.

Before he dies Arcite says,
'Now I forsake this life,
You must take Emilia
For your beloved wife.

'I ask of you but one small thing
So I can die in bliss;
Emilia please, I beg you now,
Give me one final kiss.'

And thus the doomed Arcite died,
And everyone agreed –
It was a tragedy the prince
Had fallen from his steed.

But now that he was dead it seemed
To be but common sense,
Emilia should have Palamon
By way of recompense.

The duke agreed their marriage
And then he did proclaim,
That this time, fickle fortune
Had played a subtle game.

'For it is very strange indeed
That things should end this way,
But one fact yet remains the same –
We'll have a wedding day!'

'You're banished now forever'

CYMBELINE

Way back in the mists of time
Augustus ruled in Rome
And Britain's king was Cymbeline,
Who reigned back here at home.

He ruled the whole of Britain –
But then his first wife died.
Sad Cymbeline was most distraught,
Oh, how the poor man cried!

But to console and succour him
He had three children fair:
Two boys on whom he showered his love –
A happy, boisterous pair...

And a daughter, Imogen,
The oldest of his brood;
And these three children helped to lift
His sad, despondent mood.

The little boys were very young,
Still wanting "mother's knee".
One was but a baby,
The other was just three.

But then by most unhappy chance,
On one horrendous day,
Someone crept to where they slept
And stole the boys away.

Although they searched both high and low,
Searched every inch of ground,
The two sweet, handsome, helpless boys
Were never ever found.

Cymbeline, to ease his grief –
To get another life –
Observed a decent interval,
Then took another wife.

His second marriage wasn't great –
The woman that he chose
Was no sweet, pleasant, caring type;
She was no English rose.

She was a nasty piece of work,
A scheming, plotting sort;
She brought no calm or happiness
To Cymbeline's great court.

She really hated Imogen,
She thought the girl was crass,
And treated her quite terribly –
Was unfair to the lass.

But though the queen had all this bile
And hatred in her soul,
It didn't change the fact that she
Had one determined goal.

She wished for Imogen to wed
Her own beloved boy;
This was her bold, ambitious plan,
Her very devious ploy.

For she'd been married once before,
And at that time she'd had
This son, who was called Cloten –
A most unpleasant lad.

And now she wished the boy to wed
The girl that she put down;
She thought, 'If Cymbeline should die
My son will get the crown.

'As long as those two little boys
Are never brought back here;
If they were found, it would mess up
My clever plan I fear.'

But as they say, the best laid plans
Can quickly go astray;
Things often have the tendency
To go a different way.

For Imogen was scheming too,
Plans racing through her head,
And she went off one day and got
Herself, in secret, wed.

Her husband was called Posthumus –
A really decent sort;
A scholar and a gentleman
Who'd always lived at court.

His father had died fighting,
A warrior for the cause –
In one of bold King Cymbeline's
Well-planned, but bloody wars.

His wife had then been pregnant,
And when the poor girl heard
Of how she'd lost her husband dear
And all that had occurred...

She just broke down in grief and woe;
She pulled her hair – went wild –
And only lived just long enough
To give birth to her child.

The child was friendless in the world –
A baby all alone,
But then good Cymbeline had said,
'I'll raise him as my own.'

He'd called the young babe Posthumus,
'Because this child,' he said,
'Was only born into the world
After his dad was dead.'

And so the youthful Posthumus,
And Imogen there too,
Were taught and played together;
Grew close – as children do.

So by the time they were full-grown
It is not hard to guess,
Their love was all-encompassing,
Complete – and nothing less.

To marry was the natural thing
For this young pair to do,
But it did not take long at all
Before the bad queen knew;

And then she wasted little time
Before she went to tell
King Cymbeline of what she'd learned:
You should have heard him yell.

He really went quite crazy,
And cried with bitter scorn,
'How could she go and marry
A subject lowly born!'

For though he'd raised the humble lad,
That surely was one thing –
It didn't mean the boy could wed
The daughter of a king.

He yelled at youthful Posthumus,
His words were cold and stark;
'You've pushed your luck too far this time,
You've overstepped the mark.

'You're banished now forever,
So leave fair Britain's shore.'
And then with anger in his eyes
He showed the youth the door.

The queen then said to Imogen –
She whispered in her ear –
'I will arrange a meeting
With your husband, dear.'

Whatever was her crafty game?
What was now in her mind?
She thought that if she helped the girl
She very soon would find...

That Imogen would trust her,
And then she could persuade
The girl to think her marriage
Should quickly be unmade;

And that – without permission
From the king, her dear old dad –
The marriage was unlawful;
Completely wrong and bad.

So then she could renew her aim
To get the girl to wed
Her darling son, young Cloten.
'I'll sort it out,' she said.

And so the loving pair met up
To say their last goodbyes;
They kissed, embraced and vowed their love
Amid so many sighs.

They gave each other keepsakes:
A bracelet for his wife,
A ring for Posthumus who said,
'I'll wear this band for life.'

Posthumus departed then,
He left his treasured home
And set his weary way towards
The continent – and Rome.

~ ~ ~

On arrival there he met
A group of brash, young chaps;
Fun-loving, pleasure-seeking types,
A bunch of real madcaps.

They came from different countries
And one day they were praising
The ladies of their own fair lands
In loud, exalted phrasing.

Posthumus of course joined in;
He said, 'Upon my life,
The lady fairest by a mile
Is my sweet, loving wife.'

The lad went on and on until
He said, 'She is the pick
Of all the girls in Britain now.'
He made the others sick.

The more that he continued
The more the young men said
That Posthumus was lying,
That he was off his head.

Then Iachimo, a Roman, vowed,
'However far you roam,
You won't find women to compare
With those who live in Rome.

'To think a girl from Britain
Could ever be compared
With any true-bred Roman lass –
Your judgement is impaired.'

But Posthumus was resolute;
A quarrel soon ensued,
And so a bet was struck upon,
To break this angry mood.

'I will go,' said Iachimo,
'To Britain and, once there,
Will make your so-called faithful wife
Transfer her love and care...

'To this brave Roman standing here –
I'll show your wife's not true:
As proof I shall bring back with me
Your golden bracelet too.

'And when I hand this over
You'll surely know one thing:
Your wife has been unfaithful –
So you'll give me her ring.

'And if I'm unsuccessful
I'll give you straight away
A pile of cash in payment –
So now, what do you say?'

Posthumus agreed at once –
He knew his wife was true.
'You'll never win her love,' he said,
'No matter what you do.'

~ ~ ~

So Iachimo for Britain sailed
To win the prize he sought,
And on arriving went at once
To Cymbeline's proud court.

Made welcome there by Imogen,
Because he was a friend
Of Posthumus, he nonetheless
Gave reason to offend...

For he declared he loved her,
He made it very plain;
But she repulsed him vigorously
With ladylike disdain.

He saw his cause was hopeless,
That Posthumus was right:
She was most faithful, loving, true,
Though he was out of sight.

So then he hit upon a plan,
And, though a rotten trick,
It was a most ingenious scheme,
Quite well thought out and slick.

He bribed the lady's servant –
The wily, devious fox –
To let him hide within her room,
Concealed within a box.

And, hidden in this wooden trunk
He didn't make a peep,
But waited in there patiently
Till she was fast asleep.

And then he ventured from the trunk,
And, making not a sound,
With notebook and a writing tool,
He took a look around.

He noted all the features
Of Imogen's fine room,
So when he told poor Posthumus
The lad would just assume...

He'd been within her chamber
And slept with his sweet dove;
Thus Iachimo could make the claim
That he had won her love.

And then the next thing that he did
Was silently to creep
Towards the bed, within the room
Where she was fast asleep.

And carefully and gingerly –
With just a gentle twist –
He took the golden bracelet from
Around the sweet girl's wrist.

Then like a ghost within the night,
The evil rotter slunk
Silently across the room
And got back in the trunk.

~ ~ ~

Iachimo returned to Rome,
And on arriving back
He didn't hang around but rushed
At once to the attack.

He laid into Posthumus.
He said, 'Your faithless girl
Did not take much persuading
To let her charms unfurl.'

'It can't be so,' cried Posthumus,
'It really can't be true.
I know my darling Imogen
Would never fancy you.'

But then the evil Iachimo
Described his lady's room;
Hearing this made Posthumus
Sink down in dismal gloom.

But then he brightened up and said,
'That doesn't prove a thing.
Others could have told you this.'
But then there came the sting.

For Iachimo then held aloft
The bracelet o'er his head,
And taunted Posthumus with glee;
'Know you this jewel?' he said.

'Your darling wife gave this to me.
She said there'd been a day
When it had meant a lot to her –
But now to give away...

'Was really but a little thing;
So here it is, my friend.'
The anger of fraught Posthumus
Was truly without end.

He gave the ring to Iachimo,
As he had said he would;
He had no inkling he'd been told
A truly gross falsehood.

But then, consumed by jealous rage,
He wrote to a dear friend,
And said, 'My dear Pisanio,
I wish my wife's swift end.'

He said, 'She has betrayed me
And so she now must die.'
And then he wrote to Imogen
And told her this great lie.

He wrote, 'I'm coming home to you,
I must see you somehow;
Pisanio will tell you where,
So go with him right now.'

~ ~ ~

When Imogen received the note,
She quickly said she'd go
To meet her husband, so she went
With Pisanio.

They made their way with all due haste
For Milford Haven town,
But on the way Pisanio said
With many a troubled frown...

'Your husband wants your death, but I
Cannot perform this task;
It really is a cruel request,
Not something he should ask.'

On hearing this she cried, 'I can't
Think now of coming home.'
And so she dressed up as a man
Intent on reaching Rome.

For though her husband wished her dead
She still adored him so,
And thus she set off there and then
To seek her love, her beau.

Before she went, Pisanio urged,
'Please take this phial, I pray,
For it contains a remedy
Which you may need one day.

'It is a cure for everything,
According to the queen.
She gave it to me saying
It's the best there's ever been.'

The queen detests Pisanio
Because he is so close
To Imogen and Posthumus –
She hopes he'll take a dose.

For she believes its poison –
But it is just a potion
That brings about a deathlike sleep
And stifles breath and motion.

So Imogen went on her way,
The potion in her care.
She journeyed through a forest wild,
And then got lost in there.

She stumbled round and round until –
With fear etched on her face –
She came upon a sort of house;
A very humble place.

For it was but a dismal cave,
A sorry little dwelling,
And who might live in such a home?
There was no way of telling.

With trepidation in her heart,
But trying to be brave,
She took a deep and bracing breath
And walked into the cave.

And there she found to her delight
A choice, lean side of meat;
And then without a 'by your leave'
She sat right down to eat.

The cave belonged to someone else,
But she was tired and weak,
So ate their food without a thought –
She really had a cheek.

I think an explanation
Would be in order here,
Because the owners of this home –
From hunting, now draw near.

One is called Belarius,
A man who once had been
A much respected noble at
The court of Cymbeline.

But he had falsely been accused
Of plotting highest treason:
Someone had made the whole thing up
For no apparent reason.

Belarius had been so hurt
And angry through and through,
That in a vengeful moment
He'd decided what to do.

He'd stolen Cymbeline's two sons;
His purpose was to make
The king a lonely, desperate man
And make his sad heart ache.

And this, of course, is what occurred
As we've already seen:
Cymbeline was as distraught
As anyone has been.

Belarius had brought the boys,
Oh such a naughty knave,
Into the forest – made a home,
Within the dismal cave.

And though he'd stolen these two lads
For vengeance – that alone –
He soon had learnt to care for them
And love them as his own.

He taught them lessons, how to hunt,
And fish with hook and line,
And so they grew into young men –
Both honourable and fine.

One was called Guiderius,
Arviragus was the other;
Belarius though had changed the names
Of each royal brother.

Guiderius was now renamed
As Polydore and then,
Arviragus was called Cadwal,
And so these two young men...

Had not the least suspicion of
Their high and princely worth;
They had no thought that they were each
Of noble, royal birth.

So back now to the story –
Belarius returns
With his reputed sons, and now
He straightaway discerns...

A visitor is in the cave.
'Whoever's this?' he cries.
'It surely is an angel
I see before my eyes.'

For though fair Imogen was dressed
As if she were a boy,
She still looked very comely,
Appealing, sweet and coy.

'Please don't harm me,' she called out.
'Here's money for the meat.
I'm sorry that I took so much
But I just had to eat.

'And if you choose to kill me
For taking meat today,
Then you should know, without the food
I'd be dead anyway.'

Belarius asked, 'What is your name?
And where is it you're going?'
'Fidele,' she then answered him.
They had no way of knowing...

Who she really was and how
She'd ended up right there.
'I head for Italy,' she said,
'At least that is my prayer.'

Belarius replied, 'Fair youth,
Don't hurry from our sight.
You truly are most welcome here,
So stay with us tonight.

'And do not judge us by this place
For though we seem lowborn
Who live in this damp, lowly cave,
Cut off, bereft, careworn...

'We are much more than first we seem;
I beg you, have no fear;
Come, be our guest and stay awhile,
You're very welcome here.'

So Imogen remained with them
And very quickly found,
A closeness with the brothers –
They liked having her around.

Of course, they called her Fidele –
They thought she was a boy.
They were completely taken in
By Imogen's sly ploy.

But then one day the boys declared
That hunting they would go;
Fidele said she wasn't well,
That she was feeling low.

And so they left her on her own,
But once they'd gone away,
A bright idea occurred to her
To help her through that day.

She thought, 'I'll feel much better if
I take some of the potion
Pisanio kindly gave to me.'
Of course she had no notion...

Of what the cordial contained –
The sorrow she would reap;
And drinking it she then fell down
Into a deathlike sleep.

Belarius and the brothers,
Returning – thought their guest
Must still be feeling low, and so
Was having a brief rest.

But when *he* neither breathed or moved
They cried in great confusion,
And that the lad was dead and gone
Was swiftly their conclusion.

It was such a sorry thing,
The brothers were so sad;
Just as they'd come to know him well –
They'd lost the lovely lad.

They carried Imogen with care
Into a shady glade
And lovingly, with gentleness,
There Imogen was laid.

They covered her with leaves and flowers
And said a little prayer,
Then with sad hearts and many tears
They left the body there.

But very soon the girl awoke;
She gave a little cough,
She rubbed her eyes and cleared her throat –
The drug was wearing off.

Then she exclaimed in startled tone,
'Now how did I get here?
This mound all strewn with fragrant flowers
Seems like a funeral bier.

'I thought I'd found some helpful friends,
But now it surely seems
That they were but imagined –
A figment of my dreams.'

So once again she set her path
Away from hearth and home,
To Milford Haven and from there,
She'd board a ship for Rome.

~ ~ ~

Meanwhile a war had broken out
Ferociously between
Rome's Emperor, Augustus,
And Britain's Cymbeline.

A Roman army now advanced
Right through the very wood
In which the fleeing Imogen
Unknowingly, now stood.

And with the army came a man
Of grace and courage too –
It was her husband Posthumus
Who now came into view.

But though he was surrounded
By all the Roman might,
He was determined it would be
For Britain he would fight.

And though King Cymbeline had said,
'You're banished from this land.'
It was to him that he was set
To give a helping hand.

He thought his Imogen was dead,
For Pisanio had sent
A note to say he'd killed her,
And though he did repent...

That he had caused his wife's demise,
Now nothing could be done;
He simply yearned for death because
He felt his course was run.

He'd lose his life in battle,
Embroiled in an attack,
Or Cymbeline would kill him
For daring to come back.

And so a battle then commenced
'Twixt Rome and Britain's force,
And Fortune seemed to favour Rome
As battle took its course.

Belarius and the king's lost sons
Had joined the army too;
The three of them all thought it was
The decent thing to do.

Then, with amazing bravery,
Posthumus – at the scene –
Along with old Belarius
And the sons of Cymbeline...

They turned the battle round and saved
The life of Britain's king;
It was the most astounding feat,
A really marvellous thing.

Their actions saved the battle
And put Rome's force to flight.
It was a glorious victory,
A quite amazing sight.

~ ~ ~

But what of lonely Imogen?
What happened to the lass?
Well she had been surrounded by
The Romans in a mass.

She'd then been taken prisoner
And forced to serve as page
To one of Rome's great generals
For but a paltry wage.

The fight then over, Imogen,
A *Roman* too it seemed,
Was taken prisoner by the Brits
For no-one present deemed...

She was the princess in disguise;
(Well, how were they to see?)
And so she waited there with hope
That soon they'd set her free.

And with her stood the general
Whom she'd been forced to serve.
Lucius was the general's name –
A man of steel and nerve.

And now the very Iachimo,
Who'd told such awful lies
To heartbroken Posthumus,
Stood there with downcast eyes;

For he was now a prisoner too,
And brought to Cymbeline,
And Posthumus – now taken –
Was summoned to the scene.

So they all stood there waiting for
Their fate to be made known;
Posthumus now thought for sure –
His cover being blown...

That he would soon be put to death;
It's what the king would rule.
To hope for any mercy
Would be to act the fool.

And then Belarius came in,
And with him standing there,
The two brave sons of Cymbeline –
Oh, such a handsome pair.

They came to gain their just reward
For how the three had striven,
To save the king and for the help
And service they had given.

And also with the king was found
Pisanio as well;
He was the king's attendant and
Saw all that then befell.

~ ~ ~

They waited there in silence;
Before the king they knelt,
Each with his different hopes and fears
Dividing how they felt.

Imogen gazed at Posthumus,
And saw her heart's desire.
He didn't recognise her dressed
In all her male attire.

But then she spotted Iachimo;
This man of course she knew,
But didn't know as yet he'd been
So false and so untrue:

The author of her broken heart –
But then the strangest thing,
She saw upon his finger there
Her own beloved ring.

She gasped a little to herself;
She really must learn more,
But it was hard while she remained
A prisoner of war.

Pisanio looked at Imogen
And in a tick surmised
Just who she was, despite the fact
She was so well disguised.

For he had been the one to help
Her dress up as a boy;
He'd been the willing architect
Of this her crafty ploy.

Belarius then spoke these words
In whispers to his son:
'Cadwal, is that Fidele?
I'm sure that he's the one...

'We found that day within our cave,
Who subsequently died.'
'He looks the same, without a doubt,'
His faithful *son* replied.

'If it were he, he would speak out,'
Belarius then said.
'He'd say a friendly word to us –
Fidele must be dead.'

Posthumus stood there silently,
Determined he'd not say
How he had helped to save the king
On that auspicious day.

He wished no pardon for his pains –
No kingly act of grace;
He'd welcome death and run to it,
A smile upon his face.

The Roman general, Lucius
Was first of them to speak.
It must be said he truly thought
His future looked most bleak.

'I've heard it told,' he bravely said,
'That you, King Cymbeline,
Will ransom no poor prisoners,
For vengeance must be seen.

'You sentence all you catch to death,
And so I boldly say
I'll gladly suffer death from you –
But in a Roman way.

'And I would ask but one small thing,
And beg you to engage
Your kindly virtues and to spare
This young boy here – my page.

'He is a Briton by his birth
And I must truly stress
It wasn't by his doing that
He wound up in this mess.

'He was taken prisoner
And therefore had no choice
Except to do as he was told;
He really had no voice.

'And he has proved to be as true
As any Roman lad.
The boy is kind and dutiful,
The best I've ever had.

'And yes, he served a Roman –
Though not for very long –
But I can say with certainty,
He did no Briton wrong.'

When Cymbeline took in these words
And saw his daughter fair,
Of course he didn't recognise
The girl disguised right there.

But something in her presence
Moved him in such a way
That with all kingly grace and charm
He had these words to say:

'I spare your life, young gracious boy,
And then another thing –
You may ask a favour
From me, your noble king.'

Said Imogen, 'Thank you, my lord.'
And Lucius then spoke;
He thought his page would speak for him
And save him at a stroke.

He said, 'I do not beg my life,
But know it's this you'll crave.'
She said, 'I've other work to do,
Your life I cannot save.'

The general was amazed, it's true,
By such a surly mood;
He thought her action really showed
A gross ingratitude.

Then Imogen made her request.
She said, 'I wish to know
How Iachimo came by that ring?'
He had nowhere to go.

And so he there and then confessed,
He broke into a sweat,
And then he told them how he'd lied
And all about the bet.

When Posthumus heard him confess
That Imogen was true,
He told the court just what he'd asked
Pisanio to do.

He utterly broke down and cried,
'I took the sweet girl's life.
Oh, Imogen, my only love,
Oh, Imogen – my wife!'

When Imogen saw his distress
It broke her heart in two.
She threw off her disguise and cried,
'My husband – I love you!'

Then Posthumus was quite amazed –
Could not believe his eyes;
And all the court on seeing this
Burst out in happy cries.

King Cymbeline was overwhelmed,
It filled his soul with awe.
What a gracious gift from God
To find his girl once more.

But there was more for Cymbeline
To turn his fuddled head:
Belarius stepped forward,
'I beg your ear,' he said.

And then he told the king his tale,
Of everything he'd done,
And then he said, 'Here is your boy,
And here, your other son.'

The king could not contain himself,
He knew not what to do.
Guiderius stepped forward
And Aviragus too.

The king embraced the pair of them,
His love just knew no end;
Then to Belarius he said,
'I once called you my friend...

'And it shall be so once again,
For though you were a knave,
I here and now do pardon you.'
And then the king forgave.

Then Imogen said, 'Father dear,
Will you now heed my pleas?
Will you spare General Lucius?
I'm begging on my knees.'

Cymbeline agreed and said,
'Now let all warfare cease,
And I propose that with great Rome
We shall conclude a peace.'

And thus it was, surrounded by
A flood of happy tears,
A peace with Rome was made, which then
Was kept for many years.

And so it ended happily,
But one thing must be said,
And that is to recount the fact
The evil queen was dead.

She died borne down with deep despair,
Her plans had gone astray;
But also touched by some remorse –
She thus had passed away.

And what of her son Cloten?
Well, we must truly tell,
He'd got into a fight and lost,
And was now dead as well.

So with the loss of his bad wife,
This evil, scheming queen,
There was nothing left to mar
The joy of Cymbeline.

In gratitude for how things were,
How could he ask for more?
He recognised young Posthumus
As his dear son-in-law.

And Cymbeline for many years
Stood at Britain's helm;
He ruled with great compassion
Across a peaceful realm.

Also by Richard Cuddington

SHAKESPEARE'S TRAGEDIES IN EASY READING VERSE

Richard Cuddington applies his Easy Reading Verse to Shakespeare's Tragedies. These are some of the Bard's most famous and compelling plays. Retold here in simple and engaging verse, the drama and excitement unfold with an urgency and momentum that captures the essence of the original plays.

Here the reader will meet Hamlet avenging his father's murder, Romeo risking all for his Juliet, Othello borne down with jealousy, Macbeth plotting to obtain Scotland's crown and many other colourful and doomed characters.

The sheer drama of some of Shakespeare's most memorable and highly acclaimed plays is captured here in fast moving, entertaining verse.

And when you know what each play is about you may well be encouraged to find out more about what makes these people tick by venturing into the original texts, having crept under the literary barrier and already found a way in by the back door.

SHAKESPEARE'S COMEDIES IN EASY READING VERSE

Richard Cuddington offers his readers a new approach to Shakespeare which acknowledges the Bard's stature as England's finest poet and playwright but lays aside the trappings of that greatness to reveal what made him popular with his contemporary audiences and what can still enchant us today – the stories.

Here in Easy Reading Verse the author retells the stories of Shakespeare's Comedies with clarity, humour and a modern directness. Readers will meet Shylock demanding his pound of flesh, Jack Falstaff pursuing his 'merry wives', Petruchio taming his Katherine and many other unforgettable characters who leap off the page with the immediacy of cartoon personalities.

The straightforward language with its bouncing, infectious rhythms and uncomplicated verse add pace and humour to each story as it rapidly unfolds. In this way the author makes Shakespeare less intimidating to potential readers, showing that England's greatest playwright can be fun and encouraging all who enjoy these verses to sample the rich pleasure of the original work.

SHAKESPEARE'S SONNETS IN EASY READING VERSE

Richard Cuddington's light-hearted adaptation of Shakespeare's Sonnets captures the essence of the original texts but in a way that makes them instantly accessible and understandable to the modern reader.

Originally published in 1609, many critics believe the Sonnets come closer to revealing Shakespeare the man, than any of his other works. Written in the first person, the Sonnets expose an emotional range that has given them enduring appeal.

The author now applies his straightforward Easy Reading Verse to create a fresh interpretation of the Sonnets. Here in simple and enjoyable lyrics, the mysteries of the Sonnets are unravelled, and with the original texts also contained within the book, they act as an aid in the understanding of Shakespeare's masterpieces.

CHAUCER'S CANTERBURY TALES IN EASY READING VERSE

For all its great reputation and the affection in which it is held, Chaucer's Canterbury Tales, written in 14th century Middle English, can actually be a daunting prospect to read. Richard Cuddington now steps in with a novel approach to Chaucer's famous gallery of pilgrims with their tales of chivalry, romance, courtly love, treachery, avarice, bawdiness, humour and nobility.

Whether you're new to the tales, or perhaps a teacher looking to enthuse and stimulate your students, or simply thinking of re-reading them, you will find here a thoroughly entertaining and immediately accessible way in to the storytelling genius of Chaucer in simple and amusing rhyming verse.

CHARLES DICKENS' OLIVER TWIST IN EASY READING VERSE

Oliver Twist has been a family favourite ever since Charles Dickens gave birth to his marvellous story in 1837. It has been reproduced in many ways but now Richard Cuddington applies his Easy Reading Verse to recount this famous tale.

Here are all the familiar cast of characters – brought to life in fun, uplifting narrative verse that moves along at a vibrant pace. From the moment of Oliver's birth in the Workhouse, through all his adventures at the hands of Fagin and Bill Sikes until he finally finds a new life – there is never a dull moment.

The author has previously applied his straightforward, rhythmic style to The Complete Works of Shakespeare and Chaucer's Canterbury Tales and now turns to Dickens' famous story to retell it in a way that will have great appeal to children and adults alike.

CHARLES DICKENS' A CHRISTMAS CAROL IN EASY READING VERSE

Charles Dickens' A Christmas Carol is arguably the most dearly loved Christmas story ever written – a favourite with the whole family. Whether you are one of the many fans of the story or possibly even new to the tale – you will surely enjoy this adaptation, written in fast moving, light-hearted verse. Author Richard Cuddington, who has already adapted the complete works of Shakespeare and Chaucer's Canterbury Tales into fun filled, narrative verse, now applies his rhythmic style to this famous classic. Here is Scrooge in all his miserly misery, slowly being converted from his former monstrous self into a being who really knows how to celebrate Christmas. The charming verse takes us on an unstoppable journey where we meet the Spirits of Christmas Past, Present and Future, the joyful Mr. Fezziwig and of course, the tragic but lovable figure of Tiny Tim. And on the way Scrooge dominates a tale that celebrates the joy of Christmas, encouraging a belief that we should embrace its spirit throughout the year.

KENNETH GRAHAME'S
THE WIND IN THE WILLOWS
IN EASY READING VERSE

Here is a delightful re-telling of one of Britain's best-loved books, aimed at younger children but also providing a treat for Grahame's established legion of fans of all ages. Richard Cuddington's verse rendition of Kenneth Grahame's The Wind in the Willows is the perfect introduction to a volume of stories which have enchanted generations of readers with its timeless evocation of life 'along the river bank'. All the well-known characters are here: the Mole, the Water Rat, Badger, Otter and, of course, the larger-than-life and utterly irrepressible Mr Toad of Toad Hall. The author has retained all the verve and energy of the original tales, but simplified the language to make them more accessible to the younger reader. Mole's frightening visit to the Wild Wood in the depths of winter and the colourful adventures of Toad take centre stage in bubbling rhythmic verse that drives the ebullient narrative forward so that there is never a dull moment.

www.ingramcontent.com/pod-product-compliance
Lightning Source LLC
Chambersburg PA
CBHW071213080526
44587CB00013BA/1359